"Tim Bayly's *Daddy Tried* is the best book on fathering currently in print. Bayly meticulously exegetes the biblical teachings about fathers (especially fathers in the home, but also the leaders of the church and civil governors). And he applies the biblical teachings with great clarity, frankness, and vividness. He is aware that Christian fathering is today in a terribly weak state, and he stands firmly against fashionable compromises with biblical principle. But he also emphasizes winsomely that adherence to biblical principle is another name for love. This is the book to give to our sons on the verge of becoming fathers. It will clear their heads and steel their spines."

Dr. John Frame
Professor of Systematic Theology and Philosophy
Reformed Theological Seminary

"Tim Bayly understands something about marriage and family that few writing on the subject today fully grasp, and that is the depth and destructiveness of sin. So if you are looking for biblical guidance that will do more than blow sunshine at you, I recommend that you start here."

Douglas Wilson
Pastor
Christ Church
Moscow, Idaho

"Certainly no topic demands greater attention in this culture than the responsibility of fatherhood. Fathers are essential to boys and girls—and to mothers, who depend upon them for leadership, love, and partnership in the parenting journey. Bayly catches the spirit of urgency and sets forth not only the biblical pattern for fathers but also helps his readers wrestle with the challenges of this generation. He presents a winning strategy!"

Dorothy Patterson
Professor of Theology in Women's Studies
Southwestern Baptist Theological Seminary

"The title of Tim Bayly's book, *Daddy Tried*, might suggest to some that it is a sentimental journey through a failed fatherhood. It is anything but that. Indeed, the flawed patrimony that Bayly recounts was a success. And there is nothing small about this book. In fact, its horizons are cosmic—because fatherhood is rightly understood and commended as the duty of Christian men to be House Fathers, and Church fathers, and City Fathers. This call to 'Father up!' is persistently theological (as it draws upon the relationship of the Father and the Son), intensely pastoral (as it is written sympathetically from a "chief of sinners" heart), sweetly practical (in its overflow of first-person application), and relentlessly prophetic (as the author says very hard, even harsh, things much like Joe Bayly, his father, did). Yet these prophetic utterances, in their written context, and midst the context of failed fatherhoods of our day, are words of grace. *Daddy Tried* is meant to bring about a recalibration and celebration of fatherhood in the home, the church, and the world."

R. Kent Hughes
Senior Pastor Emeritus
College Church
Wheaton, Ill.

"As a senior officer in the military, I know the importance of training and leadership. I've seen what happens when there is a lack of training and/or weak leadership, as well as the clear benefits of strong leadership and rigorous training. Our families prosper or suffer on the strength and quality of the leadership from our fathers. I have seen the effects of poor fatherhood on the young men and women who come into our Armed Forces and have struggled with my own shortcomings in raising my own four children. Tim Bayly's work is an excellent call to arms for fatherly leadership and the need for us to train ourselves, each other, and our sons to be strong, loving, and compassionate fathers and husbands who will serve and protect and fight for our families—to be strong in the faith and resolute in upholding what is good, right, and noble. It's up to us, men, to provide that leadership. Tim Bayly has helped us in this quest."

Maj. Gen. Bentley Rayburn
US Air Force (Retired)

"Tim Bayly has written a gentle yet honest book for fathers. He is so gloriously realistic about the snares and failures and yet gloriously hopeful of the good that fathers can do for their children. This is a book that offers a biblical vision of redeemed fatherhood."

Dr. Liam Goligher
Senior Minister
Tenth Presbyterian Church
Philadelphia, Pa.

"Well before I knew Tim Bayly, I knew his father, Joe Bayly. Indeed, in late 1980, I made a point of driving several hundred miles to ask Joe Bayly's counsel on a critical decision I was about to make. I still remember the wisdom he offered. So when I learned earlier this year that Tim Bayly was completing a book called *Daddy Tried*, I worried that Tim was being careless with the memory of a man whom I treasured. Tim Bayly has, after all, done radical things before! Now, however, I've read Tim's book, and I'm here to report: Tim has made me love God's Word more than ever before. Tim has convicted me of carelessness and sin in my own life. And he has prompted me to treasure the memory of his father not less, but ever so much more."

Joel Belz
Founder
World Magazine

DADDY TRIED

DADDY TRIED

OVERCOMING THE FAILURES OF FATHERHOOD

TIM BAYLY

WARHORN
MEDIA

Daddy Tried: Overcoming the Failures of Fatherhood

Warhorn Media
2401 S Endwright Rd.
Bloomington, IN 47403
WarhornMedia.com

Cover design by Ben Crum
Interior layout by Alex McNeilly. Typeset in 11/14 pt. Adobe Garamond Pro.

Printed in the United States of America
21   20   19   18   17   3   5   6   7   8

ISBN-13: 978-1-940017-09-9 (paperback)
ISBN-13: 978-1-940017-10-5 (EPUB)
ISBN-13: 978-1-940017-11-2 (Kindle)

To
Doug and Heather,
Joseph and Heidi,
Ben and Michal,
Lucas and Hannah,
Taylor and Réze

Like as a father pitieth his children, so the LORD pitieth them
that fear him.
For he knoweth our frame; he remembereth that we are dust.

Psalm 103:13–14

CONTENTS

Acknowledgments   xiii
Introduction   3

PART 1 - FATHERHOOD LOST   11

1 Father-Hunger 15
2 The Fall 25
3 The Fruit of the Fall Today 31

PART 2 - FATHERHOOD REDEEMED   43

4 God Is Love 47
5 God Disciplines His Sons 55
6 God Is Jealous 63
7 This Is My Beloved Son 69

PART 3 - FATHERHOOD RESTORED   77

8 Fatherhood in Its Proper Place 85
9 House Fathers: Fruitfulness 91
10 House Fathers: Discipline 107
11 House Fathers: Instruction 123
12 House Fathers: Love 133
13 Church Fathers 141
14 City Fathers 151

PART 4 - FATHERHOOD AND FAILURE   171

15 Bad Fathers 173
16 He Failed Gloriously 185

Notes   193
Scripture Index   201

ACKNOWLEDGMENTS

A COUPLE WEEKS from now I will be joining my wife Mary Lee and her ten siblings and their spouses at the Michigan summer home for the celebration of her mother Margaret Taylor's ninety-ninth birthday. Several times Mom Taylor has said she wants this book finished and published, so I hope it meets with her approval. There are few living souls I desire to please more.

I thank Clearnote Church, Bloomington, for allowing me time to write; the elders and pastors of our congregation for their faithful leadership and pastoral care of the flock during my absences; my brother David Bayly for helpful criticisms and the first draft of several key sections; Michael Foster and my sister-in-law Cheryl Bayly for faithful prodding; David Curell for his strategic thinking and providing me accountability; Henry and Joanna Milewski for their sacrificial gifts to help with the expenses of writing and marketing; Vern Poythress who kindly vetted several sections for faithfulness to Scripture; the Dominguez, Klint, and Taylor families for a place to work; Jürgen von Hagen for companionship during our annual writing week as well as many helpful suggestions; and Tim Wegener who, along with many others, prayed.

Then in the work of production, I am thankful for Nathan Alberson, Joseph Bayly, and Jacob Mentzel for their editorial work that made this book readable; Ben and Michal Crum for their encouragement and design; Alex McNeilly for fact checking, copyediting, typesetting, and the Scripture index; Tina Jacobson and Mark Taylor for wise counsel; and Joel Belz for being the first to jump on board.

Finally, I thank my dear Mary Lee for being the wife and mother who allowed me to become a husband, father, and pastor.

DADDY TRIED

INTRODUCTION

Yet most I thank thee, not for any deed,
But for the sense thy living self did breed
That fatherhood is at the great world's core.

George MacDonald, *Poems*

SOME YEARS BACK, when I was a new pastor, I sat in a small-town café listening to a son of the church summarize his relationship with his father: "Nothing I did ever pleased him." In his late twenties, the son was an embarrassment to his father. He was divorced with no steady job, and his children were shunted week by week from one broken home to another, with the grandparents filling in the gaps. He came to church maybe Christmas and Easter.

As we sat across the table from each other, his eyes revealed the dying embers of what once had been a flame of father-hunger—that hunger God places in the heart of every son.

None of my seminary professors had mentioned this hunger to me. At a loss to know how to minister to this deep sadness, I was silent.

Six years later another man began to attend church. He was married with a decent job and a houseful of children, but he spent weekends in bars, a hard-drinking womanizer. After attending worship for a time, he called mid-week asking me to pray that he would quit drinking. During

3

our conversation he explained that he had become exactly what his father had predicted: "My father always told me I would never amount to anything. I was going to show him wrong, but he died on me."

Back in the seventies when Harry Chapin sang "Cat's in the Cradle," the death of a child's hunger for his father seared our nation's conscience. Chapin's lament was not a solitary one. I've spent decades listening to cultural celebrities mournfully recount their father-hunger. Here's an account of a conversation with the actor and comedian David Spade:

> There were all the ingredients of a potentially happy childhood: two parents, Judy and Sam; David and two older brothers, Brian and Andy, all evenly spaced two years apart; and a nice home in Birmingham, Mich. What went wrong?
>
> "I was playing football with my dad," Spade explained in his best deadpan, mock-serious manner. "He told me to go out for a pass. He yelled, 'Go deeper! Deeper!' Then he jumped in his dune buggy and drove away."
>
> The actor waited a split second—perfect comedic timing—and then added seriously: "One day my dad just split. I was 4. It was too much pressure—three kids, a wife and a job." He paused, then added, "He would come around once or twice a year, but that was it."[1]

This is our world: fathers split, and for the rest of their lives sons and daughters mourn their abandonment.

OUR HEAVENLY FATHER

The church's earliest confession of faith is the Apostles' Creed and it begins, "I believe in God the Father Almighty, Maker of heaven and earth."

My own father—my earthly father—has been gone thirty years and I still miss him. But each Lord's Day when we recite the Apostles' Creed during worship and I stand shoulder to shoulder with my brothers and sisters in Christ confessing, "I believe in God the Father Almighty, Maker of heaven and earth," I confess I am not fatherless. No Christian is fatherless, because God is our Father.

Our earthly fathers die. If they were good fathers, it's sad and we mourn them. Yet in our grief we remember the Father Almighty promises His sons and daughters, "I will never leave you nor forsake you" (Jsh 1:5, NIV).[2]

Near the beginning of the *Catechism for Young Children*, the father or mother asks their son or daughter the question, "Why should you glorify God?" The child is taught to respond, "Because He made me and takes care of me."[3] We initiate our children into this tender love of their heavenly Father by teaching them that God the Father made them and lovingly provides for all their needs.

The book you are reading is just a simple attempt to open up this truth: God is our loving heavenly Father who made us and cares for us.

He is the only one who can fill the aching void. And our heavenly Father is the only one who can "restore the hearts of the fathers to their children and the hearts of the children to their fathers" (Mal 4:6). It is Jesus Christ who gives us this restoration. It is not optional. True Christianity always restores the bond of love between fathers and children.

This book will work to explain the origin of our failures as fathers and to heal those failures through the power of Jesus Christ. First, we will examine the damage fatherhood suffered from the Fall of man. Second, we will look at the Fatherhood of God and the Sonship of Jesus Christ as God's divine pattern for our own sonship and fatherhood. Third, we will study three kinds of fatherhood in this world, learning how to be fathers in each of those areas in such a way that we tell the truth about God the Father Almighty. And finally, we will be exhorted to press on in the work of fatherhood, not being discouraged or giving up because of our many failures.

HARD WORK AHEAD

But I must tell you that reading a book on fatherhood will not be a quick fix. I pray this book will help you, but you must be wise. So, before we move on, a few words of caution.

First, fatherhood, as we will see, did not originate with man, but God. He is the first Father. He is the archetypal Father and His name "Father" is only used for any man when he bears some resemblance to the Father Almighty. We call our earthly fathers "father" because they are made to be like the Father Almighty.

Second, this is a book for men. I make no apology for it—I'm speaking to brothers, sons, and present or future fathers.

The word "father" is a sex-specific word. Women can't be fathers—only men. Yet, the world around us is bent on destroying God's beautiful gift of sexuality. It scorns those who divide man into two sexes, male and female, and it reserves a special scorn for men who talk about men being, well, men.

Most modern education is designed to shame such ignorant notions. It works to turn men and women into fools, to educate them down and down and down until they think the work of raising children is gender-neutral "parenting" and the really successful "parent" will raise "persons" able to make "responsible choices." Principal among those responsible choices is choosing a gender identity that fits with their own personal likes and dislikes. More and more educationalists are doing their best to train the young to resist any "gender norming" pressures still lingering among the backward and ignorant folks in their church or home.

Beyond this pressure against gender norming, there is added pressure against manhood in particular—especially fatherhood. Sex-specific talk of fatherhood excludes women and that is not nice. But women are not fathers—men are. So, setting out to study fatherhood, we hear their taunts: "Who cares about fathers? In fact, who cares about men? Why should they get any special treatment? 'Fatherhood' is just a social construct left over from the oppressive patriarchy of the ancient world that justified the abuse of women and harsh treatment of children. We should be having a conversation (not listening to a monologue) about parenting (not fatherhood)."

So you see, if we are going to give ourselves to the work before us, we must get a backbone. Fatherhood is a male-only club. Fatherhood belongs to man—not woman—because God "created them male and female."

And [Jesus] answered and said, "Have you not read that He who created them from the beginning made them male and female, and said, 'for this reason a man shall leave his father and mother and be joined to his wife, and the two shall become one flesh'?" (Mt 19:4–5)

God Himself created human sexuality such that it is only two—man and woman—and His creation design designated woman to be the mother, not the father.

We can fight against it all we want, but the fact remains: biology is destiny. We don't choose our "gender." Rather, God chooses our sex. Our sex is the gift of God. It's wonderful. If we deny that sex is hard-wired and fight against it, we will be destroyed physically, morally, and spiritually. Sex is a station in life that God commands us to embrace and obey.

And this just happens to be a book for one of those sexes. Not that I mind if your wife or daughter or sister or mother reads along, as long as she remembers when the language gets a little rough that this book was not primarily intended for her.

Third, if you're like most men, your understanding of fatherhood is twisted. You didn't grow up in a godly Christian home. You've had a bad dad or no dad at all; and even if you had a good dad, he wasn't perfect. That's why you picked up this book in the first place—you want help.

If you've never had an example of healthy fatherhood in your life, there's no way to avoid having your understanding of fatherhood corrupted. So there's simply no way to avoid twisting the contents of this book.

For instance, if you've had an abusive father, when I speak in later chapters of authority and discipline, you may recoil and be tempted to stop reading. On the other hand, if you've never been disciplined you may be tempted to become the sort of father who cops a monstrous, domineering posture toward your children.

Both errors are understandable. You've never been disciplined with love and tenderness. You've never had a father whose love and authority live in perfect peace with each other. You have no earthly context from which to understand biblical fatherhood.

If this is the case with you, I plead with you to go to church—but not just any church. Go to a church where you may see and follow godly men who provide living demonstrations of healthy, masculine, biblical fatherhood; men who will bring the words of Scripture to life, correcting your past experience and present mistakes and sins. God gave you the church.

If you want to be healed and become a better father, there is absolutely no substitute for the church. She is the mother of all the faithful. Within her we will find fathers in the faith who are godly examples for us.

How important is the church, our mother? So important that I'm tempted to tell you that if you're not in a good church with good fathers you can imitate, do not read this book until you have found such a church and put yourself under the authority of godly fathers. No book can ever replace the teaching of the apostles, the breaking of bread, fellowship, and prayer (Acts 2:42) within the household of faith (Gal 6:10), the church of the living God (1 Tm 3:15).

Fourth, if reading this book inspires you to implement changes in your home—and I hope it will—be wise about it. As a father, one of your jobs is to provide stability in your home, so you must be very careful to bring your wife and children along with you as you discover new things about God and what He requires of you. Yes, you'll have to rock the boat, but do your best to rock it gently.

And speaking of changes, the first one to make is to sit down on the couch with your dear and precious wife, the mother of your children, and listen to her.

In other words, don't be a jerk. A husband who loves his wife listens to her carefully. And when he leads her, he does so having come to understand her and the desires, fears, and hopes of her heart. The man who doesn't listen to his wife doesn't love his wife. The man who makes changes in the leadership of his home without listening to his wife is a monster.

Yes, there may be many things you need to repent of. Some changes will have to be radical and you'll have to be resolute in your leadership. Some changes may even anger your wife—listening to her doesn't always mean agreeing with her. But any changes you make must come out of a context of love.

ONE LAST REQUEST

Now, before we move on, one last request. As we look at the Bible's teaching on fatherhood, please do not flinch and turn away. Thinking biblically about fatherhood will cut us deeply—each of us. We have failed.

Note that I did not write "*you* have failed" but "*we* have failed." "All have sinned and fall short of the glory of God" (Rom 3:23). You and I have sinned and it is our own hearts that we must ask the Holy Spirit to fashion into hearts fit for fatherhood, hearts that point to God the Father Almighty.

PART 1

FATHERHOOD LOST

> Yet for us there is but one God, the Father, from whom are all things and we exist for Him; and one Lord, Jesus Christ, by whom are all things, and we exist through Him.
>
> 1 Corinthians 8:6

ONE EVENING I left an elders meeting early with a terrible pain in my abdomen. Driving home I found my body stiffening each time the car went over a crack in the asphalt. Every jolt was painful.

Arriving home, I went straight to the bedroom, but as I was about to crawl into bed, a loud voice in my head yelled at me: "This is *not* the flu!"

Half an hour later I was lying on a gurney in the emergency room, waiting to see a doctor. My pain was constant and I wanted relief. When a doc came, I assumed he'd give me some drug that would take the edge off my pain.

But when the doctor finally got to me, he couldn't figure out what was wrong. Most likely it was my appendix, he said, but my symptoms weren't normal for appendicitis. He had to be sure before masking the symptoms, so I sat there unmedicated, in great pain.

Or rather, I lay there crying. Not noisily—the little boy on the other side of the curtain had that covered. Something was stuck in his ear and he screamed and screamed. He was loudly miserable while I was quietly miserable. The pain that had begun early in the evening continued on deep into the night. My dear wife was next to me, but I'm afraid I was not good company for her.

What's the point?

Generally, people in pain are impatient. They just want to take something for it. But pain is given by God to tell us something. If we remove the pain without finding its cause and working to address it, we can't be healed.

The same is true of non-physical pain.

The pain of father-hunger is all around us, shared by men and women alike. Comedians are often the guys most willing to be honest about our culture's pains, so I've developed a habit of listening to them. Somewhere in his spiel the comedian will vomit the pain of his father-hunger, and I say "vomit" because listening to stories of fathers abandoning their sons is sickening. The disease has bloody and awful themes.

The most perceptive cope by telling shameful stories about their dads, following up the stories with wry one-liners. If the stories and jokes are good enough, they make a living out of it. Cynicism may not be the only way to mask father-hunger, but it does an okay job for millions.

Masking pain won't heal us, though; we must do the hard work of diagnosis and the harder work of treatment. Pain must direct our attention to the underlying disease. Assuming God designed father-hunger to tell us something and lead us somewhere, we must ask what He is telling us and where He is leading us.

As we ask these questions, though, keep in mind that father-hunger is never new. It's as old as time. It's the result of the sins of fathers, and the sins of fathers are at the center of man's history. They stretch back domino-like to the very beginning.

So despite the temptation to feel this way, you aren't the sore thumb of history, solitary and splendid in your pain. You aren't alone.

Nor will you be able to deal with this pain by the usual means. Self-advancement won't heal you. College, grad school, or seminary won't resolve your inner conflict. Counseling won't take it away, either. Medication may dull it, but not for long. Drinking, video games, and fantasy football drafts may take the edge off for a few hours, but when you wake up, late for work, the pain will still be there.

This is my way of warning you that the next few chapters aren't going to give you quick relief. Doctors of the soul don't traffic in painkillers. Rather, they call us to look hard at our pain, trusting that it is God-given and will lead us to the disease and its cure.

CHAPTER 1

FATHER-HUNGER

He created them male and female, and He blessed them and named them Man in the day when they were created.

Genesis 5:2

I am as a child new-born, its mother dead,
Its father far away beyond the seas.
Blindly I stretch my arms and seek for him:
He goeth by me, and I see him not.
I cry to him: as if I sprinkled ashes,
My prayers fall back in dust upon my soul.

George MacDonald, *Within and Without*

"IT'S A BOY!" It took a while to sink in. A boy. Mary Lee had given birth to a boy.

Our firstborn was a five-year-old girl, so we'd had some time to get used to raising a girl. We were fine with girls. We played with Heather; we listened to her and laughed with her. She was the greatest joy we'd ever known and suited us perfectly.

But now we had a boy and I was fearful.

Oh no. What am I going to do with a boy? I don't have a clue how to raise a son.

I kept these thoughts to myself. God had given us a boy and I was afraid to tell Mary Lee how scared I was. I felt ashamed at my fear and kept it a secret from my lover. How could I admit my response to having a boy was radically different than my response to having a girl? People were people, after all.

Mary Lee and I had both been raised in godly homes, yet we were typical children of the sixties. We thought people made too much of what we condescendingly referred to as "sex roles" in marriage and family life. In the foolishness of pride, Mary Lee and I did our best to deny that from the beginning God made us male and female, and it was good.

What our denial of the meaning and purpose of sexuality meant, in practice, was that we sorted everything out by fighting. Nothing was a given due to our sexual identity—nothing other than marital intimacy, pregnancy, childbirth, and nursing the baby. But as for doing the dishes, checking the oil, cooking dinner, changing the sheets, doing the laundry, writing the checks, and balancing the checkbook, every task became a matter of negotiation.

Our pride was so awful that even walking together was tense. I wouldn't slow down and Mary Lee wouldn't speed up. It didn't occur to us that our sex—how God divided us into male and female—was a gift in sorting out who did what. As we saw it, we were way superior to all the old man/woman stereotypes. It was time to leave them behind.

But with this second child, we were six years into marriage and the hard realities of married life had been used by God in His great mercy to alter our idealism a little. To this day I remember the morning my dear brother-in-law asked me to go on a walk with him. It was the first or second year of marriage. We were up visiting Peter and Sharon on Breezy Hill Farm and, walking down the hill from the farmhouse, Peter put his arm on my shoulder and said, "Tim, God wants you to be the head of your home."

In His kindness, God used my faithful brother-in-law to say such simple words of truth. As the months and years passed, Peter's words produced great fruit. They exploded my conceit and led me down a road of repentance by which, over many years, Mary Lee and I came to love and live out loud Scripture's commands concerning man and woman, husband and wife. The road of repentance was long and winding, though, and Mary Lee was not always an eager fellow-traveler. Especially at the beginning.

So when I finally told Mary Lee how fearful I was about having a son, she was irritated: "Why do you think you can't raise a boy? How's it any different from raising a girl? We've done fine with Heather. Why are you afraid of raising Joseph?"

I crawled back into my hole with a red face and my tail between my legs. What was wrong with me? Didn't I know raising a boy was just like raising a girl?

So why was I afraid to have a son?

Because I myself didn't know how to be a man. So how on earth could I be a father to a son? What was a man? What was a son? What was a father?

As I write, it's thirty years later and our son Joseph is all grown up. Now he himself is the father of two boys. During those thirty years I've learned a lot about being a father and one of the key things I've learned is that I'm not alone in my fears. Many of us don't have a clue how to raise a son because we were never taught what manhood is. Thus fatherhood is mysterious and intimidating, particularly when we face raising a son.

Nevertheless, life goes on. Marriages are vowed. Wives get pregnant, and about half of those who are born will look to their fathers to learn the nature of manhood, sonship, and fatherhood.

Do you recognize the weight of fatherhood? Do you see the work cut out for you in becoming a father and teaching fatherhood to your son?

Likely one of the reasons we are fearful of fatherhood is that we have come to recognize the sins and failures of our own fathers and we're afraid we will repeat them. But realizing God is the Father from whom all fatherhood gets its name, we surely can't be surprised that every man ever born has failed at this glorious task. That is, if failure is defined by our heavenly Father's perfections.

There's a quote I've become fond of: "Children begin by loving their parents; as they grow older they judge them; sometimes they forgive them."[1]

If you haven't yet, may I gently say to you that it's time to forgive your father and move on to the task at hand? Soon enough your own sons will be working to forgive you. Don't worry so very much about your own children judging your fatherhood. God Himself is keeping perfect record of what we do right and wrong, the good we do and the good we fail to do. So will we step out by faith and give ourselves to the fatherhood we have been dignified with by the Father Almighty?

Yes, we will fail. But wouldn't it be better to fail while trying?

Some of my most precious memories are of my father failing while trying to be my good father.

When I was a little boy I had a brother one year older who was my perfect companion. I remember playing with him in the living room, making tents by draping blankets and bedspreads over the backs of chairs and pulling them over to the back of the sofa. Then we'd crawl under our tent and play.

Danny was my beloved older brother and I was his shadow. Where he went I always followed. What he did, I did. What games he played, I played with him. Brother and brother growing up together in peace and joy.

Then tragedy struck.

Danny was diagnosed with leukemia and one year later he died.

I was inconsolable. We had family devotions each night and I distinctly remember thinking that God could do anything He wanted and that He'd promised to answer our prayers. So each night following Bible reading when it was my turn to pray, I'd ask God to raise Danny from the dead. This was my prayer during family devotions night after night.

Think about the knife that must have cut through the hearts of Dad and Mud (our family's pet name for Mother) and my older brother and sister as Danny's younger four-year-old brother asked God to bring Danny back. Let me tell you, right now as I write I am crying. The sadness was unbearable and I wanted it over (as I'm sure everyone else did).

In a day where nothing has weight or glory, never forget that death is an enemy—a *terrible* enemy.

Seeing my own pain, Dad did his best to love me back to health.

He got an idea. He and I would carve a boat together out of a block of wood. Then we'd attach a miniature electric battery-driven motor to the boat's stern and take it to a lake and watch it putter across the water.

Dad bought a block of wood and some carving knives and took me out to the country where he and I sat on a large log and began to carve. It wasn't a one-day job. The block of wood we intended to turn into a boat was thick and long and it would take many days of carving to hollow it out and form its bow and stern.

After our first day of carving, we went home. One day later I broke out in the most awful rash. It was all over my body, but particularly high up my legs. It turns out the log we had been sitting on had been covered with poison ivy and I'd been wearing shorts, so I was oozing everywhere.

And that was the end of Dad and his son Timmy's happy time carving a boat together.

It took a while to get over my oozing poison ivy rashes in all the most tender places. To this day I have the most awful reaction to poison ivy.

What was Dad's failure? Well, for starters, he sat his four-year-old son wearing shorts down in the middle of poison ivy. Then, when the damage had been done, he gave up on carving the boat. It was a great disappointment.

About six years later, Dad and Mud lost their eldest son, Joseph. (In the interim, another son, Johnnie, had died, so Joe was their third loss.) Cheerful, kind, and gentle, kids loved Joe. He was an excellent scholar and planned on grad school and then serving the Lord in foreign missions. He and Dad were very close. Father and eldest son, you know.

Following Joe's memorial service and burial at Glenwood Memorial Gardens on a cold January afternoon, we said tearful goodbyes to our Blue Church and Delaware County Christian School loved ones, got in our car, and drove out to the Midwest where Dad had taken a new job.

Our family was in agony.

Meanwhile, Dad was on the road representing his new employer, speaking and preaching at Sunday School conventions, InterVarsity summer camps, church conferences, summer conferences, and out on the mission field. My older sister, Deborah, was the child hit hardest this time since she and Joe were inseparable, but a year and a half later

Deborah was off to the University of Illinois. This left Mud out in the country, in the middle of corn fields, with a pre-adolescent son and two toddlers. She had no friends and Dad was always gone. Mud was dying, emotionally, and so was her husband. He traveled and spoke while she gardened.

Dad was gone half the time, but even when he was home, he was gone.

One of my memories is how, when he was in town, he'd get home from work, sit in his chrome and leather recliner, reading. Then, when I'd get home, Dad would call out, "How was your day, Tim?" and I'd answer, "Fine, how was yours, Dad?"

He'd answer, "Fine," and that was that.

Once or twice I tried to break the pattern: "No, Dad, really; how was your day? What happened? What did you do?"

My attempts to escalate our intimacy were useless. In fact, worse than useless: as far as Dad was concerned, I'd gone off the reservation. My questions fell to the ground and lay there stinking.

One time I tried to take a besetting sin to him for his counsel and it is telling that I used Mud as my intermediary. I asked her to ask him for me what he thought I should do about the sin. A couple days later Mud reported Dad had told her to tell me there are some things a man has to figure out for himself.

COVERING A FATHER'S FAILURES

You know, speaking of Dad's failures, the Bible records a key moment in the life of Noah and his sons that we should consider:

> Then Noah began farming and planted a vineyard. He drank of the wine and became drunk, and uncovered himself inside his tent. Ham, the father of Canaan, saw the nakedness of his father, and told his two brothers outside. But Shem and Japheth took a garment and laid it upon both their shoulders and walked backward and covered the nakedness of their father; and their faces were turned away, so that they did not see their father's nakedness.
>
> When Noah awoke from his wine, he knew what his youngest

son had done to him. So he said, "Cursed be Canaan; a servant of servants he shall be to his brothers." He also said, "Blessed be the LORD, the God of Shem; and let Canaan be his servant. May God enlarge Japheth, and let him dwell in the tents of Shem; and let Canaan be his servant." (Gn 9:20–27)

When I told the stories of my dad's failures just above, was I not doing precisely what Ham did? Why is it right for me to write about my dad's failures, here? Dad can't defend himself. Should I not honor my father?

It may be wrong, but here's my reasoning in thinking it's good and necessary—and maybe, even, that if Dad were present, he'd approve.

It is very easy to fall into the temptation of thinking the only sons who can become good fathers are those who had good fathers. But your dad wasn't perfect and neither was mine. Which is to say, there are no good fathers. Remember Jesus' response to the rich young ruler?

As He was setting out on a journey, a man ran up to Him and knelt before Him, and asked Him, "Good Teacher, what shall I do to inherit eternal life?" And Jesus said to him, "Why do you call Me good? No one is good except God alone." (Mk 10:17–18)

Further, when Jesus was speaking specifically about our fatherhood, do you remember what He said about us?

Now suppose one of you fathers is asked by his son for a fish; he will not give him a snake instead of a fish, will he? Or if he is asked for an egg, he will not give him a scorpion, will he? If you then, being evil, know how to give good gifts to your children, how much more will your heavenly Father give the Holy Spirit to those who ask Him? (Lk 11:11–13)

According to our Lord Jesus, every father is properly described as "being evil."

We have not been glorified yet. We are being sanctified. We are being made holy, but it's a long and winding and painful road.

That's the nature of the life of faith. A Christian is a man who, by faith, has committed himself to failing in the right direction.

As the years have passed, I've come to love my dad most for these very failures. It's not that I no longer wish we'd finished carving the boat. It's not that I don't still feel some sadness that Dad and I didn't talk about my sin.

Rather, it's that, even in these failures, I learned the nature of the love of a Christian son for his godly, kind, intelligent, thoughtful, wise, and tender Christian father.

It wasn't that Dad sat me down in poison ivy, but that Dad had an idea that carving a boat together would heal my grief. And maybe his, too.

Daddy tried.

But what about his avoidance of intimacy? What about his road trips after his eldest son Joe died?

Looking back on it, I see how easy it would have been for Dad to give in to his grief and leave his wife and children entirely. The divorce statistics for parents who lose a child or children to death are much debated, but clearly the loss of one child is a stress many couples never recover from—let alone three children.

Dad and Mud persevered, and I've come to realize that Dad and Mud both had such gaping wounds that it was a victory they stayed together at all. Their commitment to marriage was faith. For some time theirs was a very weak faith—and therefore theirs was a far greater faith than I've ever been called by God to exercise myself. Who am I to judge my father?

No, I will not judge my father. I will love him. I will forgive him. I will pray that my heavenly Father never calls on me to demonstrate the faith He called on my father and mother to demonstrate.

It took about a decade, but Dad came home in time for my two younger brothers to enjoy him fully. My image of my younger brothers, David and Nathan, as they grew up, was Nathan sitting in Dad's lap or over on the fireplace next to Dad talking with him while David lay on the floor behind Dad's chair reading. It was a tender sight. Beyond David and Nathan, though, Dad and Mud healed together and I had the full benefit of Dad's wisdom and counsel as I got married, as Mary Lee and I had our first two children, and as I entered the pastorate.

When Mary Lee and I had our tenth wedding anniversary, Dad and Mud offered to come up to Wisconsin and take care of our two children, Heather and Joseph, while Mary Lee and I used two nights they gave us down in Chicago at the Marriott on North Michigan Avenue. Dad offered to preach for me, and, before Mary Lee and I left, I took a small Post-it note and wrote, "I love you, Dad," and stuck it to the top of the pulpit so when he began preaching he'd see it.

You can see how much I love my dad, right?

Is it because he was perfect? Is it because he did everything right?

No, it is because, sinner though he was, I hope to rise to his level of godliness before I die. And I even dare to think that the places he did fail us are the very places God will use in my life to help other fathers become better fathers. Beyond that, I've spent much of my time in the pastorate loving men and calling the other pastors and elders I work with to love men, also. Men drowning in father-hunger. How could I have seen it if I'd not felt it myself? And there's no question much of my commitment to help these men, and to get other men to help them, comes from my memory of those years after Joe's death when Dad was gone.

DON'T DIE A VICTIM

Recently, I was exhorting a man in his late fifties. I pointed out that he'd spent his life being bitter about hurts suffered in the past, and that if he didn't repent of his bitterness, he'd die a victim. What a faithless thing that is, to die feeling sorry for ourselves because of our father's failures.

Of course our fathers were failures. So were their fathers. And their fathers' fathers before them. Fact is, we can trace our own fathers' failures all the way back through history, then back through Scripture itself to the beginning of time.

But if you are a believer in Jesus Christ, you are the adopted son of the Father from whom all fatherhood gets its name, so you have nothing to complain about, really. He is perfect. He never fails us. He is not fickle. He doesn't avoid intimacy. He's a friend who sticks closer than any brother.

And He knows our weakness.

As we begin our work growing in fatherhood, let's have this statement of our heavenly Father's character fixed firmly in our minds:

> The LORD is merciful and gracious, slow to anger, and
>   plenteous in mercy.
> He will not always chide: neither will He keep his anger for
>   ever.
> He hath not dealt with us after our sins; nor rewarded us
>   according to our iniquities.
> For as the heaven is high above the earth, so great is His mercy
>   toward them that fear Him.
> As far as the east is from the west, so far hath He removed our
>   transgressions from us.
> Like as a father pitieth his children, so the LORD pitieth them
>   that fear Him.
> For He knoweth our frame; He remembereth that we are dust.
> As for man, his days are as grass: as a flower of the field, so he
>   flourisheth.
> For the wind passeth over it, and it is gone; and the place
>   thereof shall know it no more.
> But the mercy of the LORD is from everlasting to everlasting
>   upon them that fear Him, and His righteousness unto
>   children's children;
> To such as keep His covenant, and to those that remember His
>   commandments to do them.
> (Ps 103:8–18, KJV)

CHAPTER 2

THE FALL

. . . the son of Shem, the son of Noah, the son of Lamech, the son of Methuselah, the son of Enoch, the son of Jared, the son of Maha- laleel, the son of Cainan, the son of Enosh, the son of Seth, the son of Adam, the son of God.

Luke 3:36–38

Your first forefather sinned,
And your spokesmen have transgressed against Me.

Isaiah 43:27

SO YOU WANT to blame someone for the state of fatherhood to- day? The commissioner of the NFL? Hillary Clinton? Abraham or King David? Your own dark-hearted grandpa?

Go back further—all the way back to the real source.

Blame Adam. He is the source of man's rebellion against God the Father Almighty. Through his rebellion, Adam corrupted the image of God in man, ruining man's fatherhood.

Eating the fruit of the one tree forbidden him, Adam sinned, and because of that one sin, every man, woman, and child across human history has been conceived in sin, lives in bondage to that sin, and is subject to God's judgment. You are depraved. You, dear man, are a wicked sinner.

In other words, contrary to what your grandmother always said, you are not a nice boy.

The New England Primer was the first textbook printed in America and it taught the letters of the alphabet by short poems. Here's the first, teaching the letter *A*:

> In Adam's fall,
> We sinned all.

Follow your family tree back generation after generation. Follow it across the Atlantic to Africa or Europe; go back to the Middle Ages, then the ancient world; go back and back and back until you come to Noah and his family at the time of the Great Flood; finally, travel back to Adam himself where you will find the only explanation that makes any sense of your father-hunger and father-failure.

There at the very beginning you will find that you are not a sinner because you sin. Rather you sin because you're a sinner, and you're a sinner because of God's judgment upon our federal head, Adam. His guilt is our guilt, his fall our fall, his death our death, his judgment by God our judgment by God.

ADAM'S FALL

If you're reading this book, you're likely a Christian and you know what happened in the Garden. But have you really thought about it?

Picture the most beautiful, peaceful garden you've ever seen. That was the beauty of the Garden of Eden.

Think of it: a beautiful and fruitful garden; a loving Adam; a beautiful and fruitful Eve. Adam and Eve together, naked and unashamed. What more could Adam want? It was perfection. It was holiness. It was peace. This was the Garden of Eden.

Then something went terribly wrong.

Taking a serpent's form, Satan sought to lead Adam and Eve, the

crown of God's creation, into the same rebellion against God he himself
had chosen. And in his devious brilliance, he aimed at the weaker vessel,
Eve.

Being herself deceived, Eve became Satan's emissary, enticing Adam
to eat the fruit with her. Here's what the Bible scholar E. J. Young says
about Adam's failure:

> In hearkening to the voice of his wife Adam had forfeited his po-
> sition as the crown of creation and the head of the wife, and had
> placed himself into the subordinate position which belonged to the
> woman. Instead of showing her the way in which she should walk,
> he had yielded to her direction and sinned against God.[1]

There's one point that needs to be nailed down so tightly we can't
escape it. God faulted Adam for listening to his wife and following her
into sin (Gn 3:17). Adam was the head of his wife, but their relationship got flipped upside down when Eve led and Adam followed. Eve's
superior became her subordinate. He listened to her voice and followed
her into sin.

God's progression is straightforward: God commands Adam. Then
Adam himself obeys and leads his wife into obedience. Together they
honor the Father through obedience to His Word, and thus Satan is
defeated.

Satan reverses God's order: Satan entices Eve. Then Eve rebels against
God, urging Adam to do the same. Adam listens to Eve and himself rebels against God.

One progression is right side up, the other upside down.

Just like that, it was over. Over for peace and beauty. Over for intimacy without shame. Over for unity between God and man, man and
woman. Over for every man, woman, and child down to this present
day. All over.

You ask what this has to do with fatherhood?

Adam's rebellion was the repudiation of God's Fatherhood. And having turned his back on God the Father Almighty, Adam repudiated his
own fatherhood by refusing to accept responsibility for himself and his
wife. Note what happens when God comes to the Garden after Ad-

am's fall. Eve sinned first, but God goes directly to Adam, asking him, "Where are you?" (Gn 3:9).[2]

Adam answered, "I heard the sound of You in the garden, and I was afraid because I was naked; so I hid myself" (v. 10).

God responded, "Who told you that you were naked? Have you eaten from the tree of which I commanded you not to eat?" (v. 11).

Adam answered, "The woman whom You gave to be with me, she gave me from the tree, and I ate" (v. 12).

Men, I hope we recognize ourselves in Adam's response. God made Adam head of the woman. God placed on Adam the obligation and authority to tend and protect His creation. Yet Adam chose to rebel against his Father above and to be a passive-aggressive abdicator against his wife, children, and descendants below.

Is there one of us who has the slightest problem recognizing his father, his sons, and himself in this account of the federal head of our race?

"In Adam's fall, we sinned all."

Fatherhood has never been the same.

OUR REJECTION OF FATHERHOOD

Adam sowed the wind and every generation since has reaped the whirlwind. Adam refused to submit to God the Father, instead submitting to his wife who herself had submitted to Satan; and ever since, rebellion reigns.

Now we live in an evil day in an evil time. Everything is upside down and fatherhood is on life support. We think nothing of children being bastards—the word is almost dead. Single women and lesbians get artificially inseminated with not a care in the world about their child growing up without a father.

Who needs a father? Isn't a mother enough? Can't the child take her mother's name, instead? What are fathers good for, anyway? They divorce your mother. They sit and watch television. They play video games through the evenings and weekends. They berate and hound your sons. They molest your daughters. Who needs a father?

But it doesn't stop there. It continues inexorably on to God because fatherhood descends from Him and points back to Him.

Who needs God? What's He done for me, anyhow? Did He give me a father who loved me? Did He give my mother a husband who was faithful to her and provided for her and their children? Did He protect me from my stepfather? Did He keep my father from walking out on my mother? What's He done for me, anyhow—in fact, what's He done for anyone?

You expect me to believe in God the Father?

Get serious.

In lockstep solidarity with our first father, Adam, we choose rebellion against our Father in heaven and we despise the calling of earthly fatherhood. Fathers who despise God's Fatherhood inevitably abdicate their responsibilities: they do not provide, they fail to protect, they do not lead their wives and children into the safety of righteousness, and what happens?

Women pick up the pieces. Yet it's hard for woman to do the work and bear the responsibility God delegated to man. By divine design, woman is unsuited to the authority and responsibility God placed in man by His order of creation.

Now where are we?

Man is in rebellion, woman is deceived, and children—if not murdered in the womb—are left in a world of wolves, defenseless.

God? God who? Where's God? Why's God? Who needs God? No, I won't pray to Him—and certainly not call Him "Father"! I don't need a father!

Adam traded the fatherhood of God for the fatherhood of Satan, and that's made all the difference. Since his fall every man is born into slavery to the devil, and the devil has become man's father. This is the meaning of King David's declaration, "in sin my mother conceived me" (Ps 51:5). And here we remain, today: murderous, lying rebels. Lovers of evil rather than good. Preferring Satan's fatherhood to God's.

Since Adam's fall, the only way for God to be restored as our Father is for us to be born again of the Holy Spirit. Only those born again become adopted sons of God whose hearts cry out "Abba! Father!" (Rom 8:15; Gal 4:6).

But we've not finished probing the depths of the Fall, and what it means in our day and age.

CHAPTER 3

THE FRUIT OF THE FALL TODAY

The fathers have eaten sour grapes,
And the children's teeth are set on edge.

Jeremiah 31:29

THE HISTORY OF SCIENCE scholar Jacob Bronowski had a best seller a couple decades ago called *The Ascent of Man*. Of course, with lots of pictures and such a title, the book was a best seller.

Think about that title. *The Ascent of Man*.

It is modern man's conceit that "humankind" is getting better and better. The world religiously believes that man descended from apes and continues evolving—which is to say progressing or ascending—to this very day.

Yet this is the opposite of the history recorded in God's Word.

We've talked about the first man, Adam, and his sin and failure. Well, the apple didn't fall far from the tree. Cain followed his father's path of the blame game. He attempted to cover his sin by denying responsibility for his brother: "Am I my brother's keeper?" (Gn 4:9).

Welcome to the family of Man in which alienation is celebrated as autonomy. This is the first family of the human race.

Two chapters later, God records for us the wickedness of man prior to the Flood. Who can ever forget this summary of man's condition?

Then the Lord saw that the wickedness of man was great on the earth, and that every intent of the thoughts of his heart was only evil continually. The Lord was sorry that He had made man on the earth, and He was grieved in His heart. (Gn 6:5–6)

Did you read that? "Every intent of the thoughts of his heart was only evil continually."

Of course that sort of wickedness ended with the Flood, right?

Well, yes, except . . . remember Sodom, the city full of men hell-bent on raping the angels God sent? And Lot who offered the Sodomites his daughters to sate their lust? Remember Lot's wife—what happened to her, and why? Also Lot's daughters—those same daughters he offered to the Sodomites? How the daughters conspired to get their father drunk and took turns having sex with him? And what about Abraham who twice passed his wife off as his sister, sending her to join the harem of another man? And Isaac who passed his wife off as his sister just as his father had before him? Jacob who was a deceiver? Jacob's sons who sold their brother Joseph into slavery? And what about the entire generation of Israel God condemned to death in the wilderness due to their complaining and immorality and idolatry? How about the kings of Israel and Judah? Ahab? Manasseh? Good King Hezekiah—the king who was relieved that judgment on his sins from the hand of God would fall on his children after he was dead, and not on himself?

Are those the happy-days-are-here-again we're looking for?

Finally, what about that "man after God's own heart" (1 Sm 13:14), King David? Did he preserve his family, his sons and daughters, from the corruption of the Fall?

We must face the fact that this man David was indeed a man after God's own heart, but he committed adultery with Bathsheba; and then to cover it up he murdered Bathsheba's husband, Uriah (2 Sm 11). That's King David.

What about David's children? Amnon who raped his sister, Tamar (2 Sm 13)? Absalom who solicited rebellion against his father (2 Sm 15–18)? And what does Scripture record concerning King David's fatherhood in relation to his son, Adonijah?

His father had never crossed him at any time by asking, "Why have you done so?" (1 Kgs 1:6)

This chapter is titled "The Fruit of the Fall Today." Right about here, readers might want to pull me aside to explain how different Bible-believing Christians today are from Cain and Lot and Jacob and David. You may find yourself saying:

Don't lump us in with them. We're different. We don't have that kind of sin in our church. You seem to have an awfully negative view of the power of the Gospel. Yes, of course we fail. We all sin. We all make bad choices. Nobody loves their wife and children the way they ought to. But we live by grace. The answer to failure isn't guilt, but seeing ourselves the way God sees us. We live in the days after Christ has come, and we are hidden in Christ! We are seated in the heavenly places! That's what the Bible says! Jesus came to save us from all our feelings of guilt. We're free! We can't do anything to earn His approval. Jesus loves us just the way we are!

Well yes, of course. The man who lives by faith in Jesus Christ is seated in the heavenlies. Of course he lives by grace.

Still, there's all that sin and failure in Scripture—much of it by God's people—so it must have a point. Remember that "all Scripture" is "profitable for teaching, for reproof, for correction, for training in righteousness; so that the man of God may be adequate, equipped for every good work" (2 Tm 3:16–17). All Scripture.

So what's the point of that massive body of testimony to the destructive results of the Fall among the people of God so meticulously recorded throughout Scripture?

TO KNOW OURSELVES

As I've pointed out already, before we are able to heal a disease we must do a proper diagnosis. Often the process of that diagnosis is long and painful—even humiliating. But there's no way around it. Some blood work, a CAT scan, maybe a day of liquids followed by a colonoscopy; or into the examining room and clothes off, please; this is the stuff necessary to diagnose our physical diseases.

It's not much different with our spiritual diseases. Of course we can choose to go to a church where the pastor never forces us to look at our teeth and our gums, where he never requires us to have an endoscopy or to get on the examining table. But what's the use? Where will that get us—sitting under a preacher who never preaches to our sin and our conscience?

Won't you look at yourself honestly as we proceed?

A FATHER'S INSTRUCTION

I grew up with a dad who never stopped quoting Scripture to his children, including its warnings; and perhaps more than any other warning, this one from the prophet Jeremiah:

> The heart is deceitful above all things,
> And desperately wicked;
> Who can know it?
> (Jer 17:9, NKJV)

Dad's repetition of the Bible's warning marked the beginning of my understanding of the human heart. Now, however, I have thirty years behind me during which I have been privileged to hear many confessions of sin; thirty years during which, in my own limited ability, I have sought to help bear sin's awful pain and join sinners in prayers of repentance and faith.

All this is the work of a pastor feeding and guarding his flock, and it's from such experience that I have come to see and feel, with tears, the fruit of the Fall today. Especially in the failures of fathers.

PASTORAL WORK TODAY

Let me give several examples. The following are not cherry-picked. They're simply fathers and their households who come to mind as I seek to demonstrate to you how pervasive and tragic the fruit of the Fall is right now, both inside and outside the church. I'm choosing to omit some of the most awful sins that my elders and fellow pastors, my wife and I, have cried and prayed over in the past few years.

Two junior high school boys wandered into the church one day. I'd never met them before and they had no previous experience with the church I served at the time. It was a small town and they wondered what was inside, so they walked in and knocked on my office door.

I greeted them and we began to get to know each other. After several minutes of small talk, I began to speak to them of God. Both boys responded that they didn't believe in God. Even thirty years ago and wet behind the ears, I knew enough to say, "So neither of you have a father at home, do you? And I'll bet you're angry at your dads."

One of the boys turned to the other and said, "Wow! How did he know that?" The lives of this age are defined by father-repudiation and father-hunger—both at the same time.

A college freshman came into my office and asked me what to do when he went home for Thanksgiving. An adopted child, throughout his childhood his older brother raped him. Going to college had provided relief, but now he was headed home for Thanksgiving and he was terrified his brother would start in sodomizing him again. Where was his father?

There was the sophomore active in Campus Crusade who went home for Christmas, pregnant. She'd had sex with a man also active in Cru and neither of them wanted to murder their baby.

The story of her journey home came to me weeks later, in February after she'd returned to school from Christmas break. She set up an appointment and entered my office with a friend. She was in obvious grief as she confessed her sin of fornication. She explained how she had confessed her fornication to her father and mother when she arrived home for Christmas. Then, between sobs, she told a heartbreaking story of how her father and mother had responded by telling her they wouldn't allow her to have her baby. They told her to abort her child.

She refused, so throughout Christmas break she suffered constant threats and enticements pressuring her to shed her baby's blood.

She stood strong in her godliness and repentance, and refused.

Finally her dad told her he would not pay for any more college until she had the abortion. He would not allow her to return to college until her baby was dead.

After weeks of resisting her dad's command, she finally gave in. And now she sobbed: "My baby is dead! I killed my baby!"

There was a family whose father browbeat and intimidated his wife and children. Gentle and soft-spoken in public, at home he was a psychological, emotional, and spiritual monster.

But a sexual monster, to boot: at least one of his children—his little daughter—grew up being raped by him, day after day, month after month, year after year.[1] At church he waged conscientious warfare with aspects of his pastor's theology while at home he conducted the family business fraudulently, living primarily off his wife's earnings.

There was the father who became depressed when new owners took over the business he worked for, so he killed himself leaving his bloody body for his wife to find and his daughters to mourn.

There was the grandfather who visited his children and grandchildren frequently. During those visits it was his habit to go to his children's homes and pick up his grandchildren, taking them back to the hotel where he'd molest them. He did this to most of his grandchildren, but it was years before it came out into the open. When it did, all he could talk about was his desire to have a good relationship with his family. He went on and on telling them how Jesus had forgiven him—he knew this beyond any shadow of a doubt, he said. Then he'd explain that they and their children needed to recognize their bitterness as the sin it was, repent, and forgive him. He was an upstanding member of his evangelical church and he held a responsible position in society.

There is the father who didn't discipline his children. Despite years of exhortation and admonition from his pastors and elders calling him to discipline his sons, he remained proud and unteachable. Instilling the same attitude in his children, he led them down a path so awful that I won't put it down here in writing.

There are the men whose abdication and sin produced sons who despised fatherhood and manhood, and thus went on to embrace effeminacy. There was the father whose wife wanted a daughter—not a son—and that father allowed his wife to raise their son as if he were a daughter. When he was a boy, the mother made him wear frilly dresses. By the time I knew him, he was middle-aged and driving into the city where he would pay young boys to let him sodomize them. He too was a member of an upstanding, large evangelical church and he held a responsible position in the world.

There was the man whose son was sexually abused by an older boy in the neighborhood. When his son told him what the neighbor boy had done, the boy's father responded by doing nothing. He was a seminary professor ordained to the pastorate and he did nothing. Is it any surprise the son later became a child molester himself?

There was the woman who would show up at church Sunday morning with obvious signs of having been abused. Her sons made fun of her, tormenting their mother in front of the entire congregation by throwing toys over the top of her head, playing keep-away as she made half-hearted attempts to control them. As this went on, elders sat nearby doing nothing, leaving this poor woman to her husband's abuse and her sons' humiliations.

There were the two couples at the center of a small church who were best friends with each other. Their children were best friends also. It was obvious to anyone who saw them together that the husband of one couple and the wife of the other were committing adultery, but no one confronted them. The whole world knew, but not one person in the church admitted it or was willing to confront it.

The consequences of their adultery in the lives of their children have been catastrophic.

We could continue, but one last word—this one from an elder grieving over the molestation of his young daughters by a member of his extended family. He said,

> I've been in elders meetings for almost ten years and there's never been a single mention of child molestation, abuse, or incest. Not one! Now that my own children have been molested and I've learned the truth of how common this is, I'm horrified. It must have been happening in our church, but our pastor and elders were clueless or silent.

Elders and pastors who go for ten years without hearing of or discussing (not to mention rolling up their sleeves and pants legs as they work to help) even a single case of child abuse, molestation, or incest are church fathers who have failed to love their flock. It ought never to be the case that churches in America today claim to have fewer crimes and sins against love than churches of past generations of the people of God. Do you know what the prevalence of incest and child molestation is in our society today? If you know, do you think it's less among Christians? Homeschoolers? Christian patriarchal homeschoolers? Christian patriarchal agrarian homeschoolers who are Bible-believing? Baptist? Presbyterian?[2]

WE HAVE MET THE SINNERS AND THEY ARE US

In 1 Corinthians 5, the Apostle Paul rebukes the Corinthians for being proud while there was incest within their congregation:

> It is actually reported that there is immorality among you, and of a kind that is not found even among pagans; for a man is living with his father's wife. And you are arrogant! (vv. 1–2, RSV)

You see? Men and women haven't changed. Sin hasn't changed. God's covenant people haven't changed. As with the church of Corinth, as with all the sinners throughout the Old and New Testaments, so with the churches and households of Christians today. We are proud while not removing the incest, child molestation, adultery, fornication, covetousness, swindling, idolatry, reviling, and drunkenness within our congregations.

You're proud that these sins aren't within your church?

So were the Corinthians. Or that's what they would have told you. They were monkeys who saw no evil, heard no evil, did no evil.

Along with our church's pastors, elders, and older women, what Mary Lee and I often see in the eyes of our young men and women is fear and pain. Sometimes it's grief over a dead sibling murdered by their parents through abortion. Their father or mother told them of it and they can't see why they should be alive themselves when their parents murdered their brother or sister.

More often, though, the fear and suffering in their eyes is the result of sexual abuse, and in such cases it's extremely difficult to work to restore their trust of any father, whether church fathers, home fathers, or God the Father Almighty. They've given in to fear.

Do you see the evil and suffering in your own congregation?

Perhaps you'd rather not? *This isn't normal,* you say; *most children grow up in nice families with good fathers and mothers, and siblings who treat them with respect.*

Really? So the Bible's accounts of the homes of the patriarchs, of Israel's kings, and of the Corinthian church are only there to illustrate exceptions to the rule?

As I said, I've now been in pastoral ministry for most of my life, and for the past twenty-four years my wife and I have been serving in a university community.

If they love Jesus by feeding His sheep, do you know what pastors and elders in college and university communities spend their time doing? We spend our time hearing the confessions and bearing the pain and shame of young men and women who have just escaped their homes for the first time and are finally free to talk to someone about what they suffered in those homes. I've heard a number of confessions from souls who grew up in homes every bit as wicked as the incestuous home at the center of the Corinthian church.

More often than not, they are homes that claim to be Christian. They have conservative translations of Scripture—say, the ESV or the NASB—sitting on the end table next to the couch. Mother teaches Sunday school and Father is an elder or a deacon. The whole family goes to church together each Sunday. Their pastor preaches sermons on God's grace and everyone in attendance smiles, smells good, and dresses tastefully.

Christian homes. Christian fathers and mothers. The children all baptized, taking communion, and writing relatives to ask for support for their short-term mission trips. Sneak into a subset of those homes under cover of darkness, though, and what you'll find will scar you.

NO ONE WANTS TO HEAR IT

You say you don't want to hear about it?

Well of course not—who does? Who wants to stand in emotional or spiritual solidarity with those who suffer in such ways? Who wants to care for those who have confessed committing those awful sins, especially if his or her victims were women and children?

A young woman came into my office but wouldn't sit down. She stood just inside the door and was deathly afraid. Very softly she told how her brother had molested her throughout her childhood. (There was no mother in the home.) After years of suffering, she summoned the courage to tell her aunt and her aunt directed her to their priest. So she went alone to her priest, hoping for a shepherd to protect her from the wolf. The priest turned out to be a more ravenous wolf himself. He responded to her plea for help by propositioning her to have sex with him.

This is the world we live in.

Do you think such men are unusual? That it's the rare Christian man who gets involved in children's ministry or youth work in order to gain access to boys and girls whose parents are trusting of church leaders? Do you think authorities turning blind eyes to these crimes are the exception to the rule?

If so, you've made the choice to live in the land of the blind.

HOPE LIES AHEAD

The fruit of Adam's rebellion against God the Father is woven through the pages of Scripture. And it is equally woven through the fabric of our own lives and the lives of our loved ones.

Just like our father Adam, we too turn from fatherhood to embrace rebellion. The world today is the same fallen, father-hating, and father-hungry world of yesterday.

But that's only half the story. God has not abandoned us to our sin.

PART 2

FATHERHOOD REDEEMED

> . . . for I have chosen him to be a son to Me, and I will be a father to him.
>
> 1 Chronicles 28:6

IN HIS AUTOBIOGRAPHY, Augustine makes this confession:

> Thou hast formed us for Thyself, and our hearts are restless till they find rest in Thee.[1]

All our restless, aching father-hunger points to the absence of the intimacy and love for which God made us. He made us for Himself and our hearts are restless until they find their rest in Him. Our father-hunger is Father-hunger.

My wife Mary Lee and I have twenty-one grandchildren and three of our grandsons are adopted. If you or other families in your church have adopted, you know how precious these sons and daughters are.

Think of adoption from the perspective of the child. Think of going from having no father or mother to having a father and mother who feed you, clothe you, bathe you, discipline you, carry you when you're tired, read to you, play with you, and tuck you in at night with hugs, kisses, and prayer. Think of having no one to love you, then suddenly having a father and mother who love you until death and make you equal to their own children in everything—absolutely everything, including an inheritance.

When an orphan is adopted, his life is changed. Nothing is the same; all things have become new. This is what our heavenly Father has done for everyone who has turned from his sinful rebellion and trusted in His Son, Jesus.

Except we weren't innocent orphans. We were rebels, completely deserving the wrath of God and Hell's torments. Think back on the previous chapters, think of your own sin, and consider what you truly deserve. And yet, this is what God says:

> But when the fullness of the time came, God sent forth His Son, born of a woman, born under the Law, so that He might redeem those who were under the Law, that we might receive the adoption as sons. Because you are sons, God has sent forth the Spirit of His Son into our hearts, crying, "Abba! Father!" Therefore you are no longer a slave, but a son; and if a son, then an heir through God. (Gal 4:4–7)

Jesus, the Son of God, died not only to save us from God's wrath, but to make us the adopted sons of God. To reconcile us to God the Father. To heal our Father-hunger.

As radical and wonderful as it is for orphans, adoption is infinitely richer and deeper for us. It isn't easy to get our minds around the glory of God's adoption of us. It's even harder to get our minds around the fact that, being God's sons, we are made Jesus' brothers and share all the rights of inheritance with Him. Yet this is the meaning of our adoption by our heavenly Father. Scripture describes the radical nature of this change: "Therefore if any man be in Christ, he is a new creature: old things are passed away; behold, all things are become new" (2 Cor 5:17, KJV).

God has adopted the believer as His own son, and now He is not simply the Father Almighty, but He is *our* Father in heaven. *Our Father* who never leaves or forsakes us.

And how tender He is with us:

Just as a father has compassion on his children,
So the LORD has compassion on those who fear Him.
For He Himself knows our frame;
He is mindful that we are but dust.
(Ps 103:13–14)

He understands us. He disciplines us. He rebukes us. He leads us to green pastures and still waters. He restores our souls. He forgives us. He does not always chide us nor does he keep His anger forever. He teaches us. He feeds us. He prepares a home for us in Heaven.

He knows us *and* He loves us.

This is Fatherhood redeemed. Redeemed despite our rebellion, despite our corruption, despite our sin. Redeemed by the Father Almighty through the work of His beloved Son.

Dear brother, that aching hole of father-hunger within you is healed when, through the blood of God's Son, your restless heart is restored to the Father Almighty, and to His household of faith. From then on, your life is no longer defined by how bad your earthly father was.

As we come to know God as our heavenly Father, we learn the true nature of fatherhood. Buried with Christ, He made us holy and makes us holy, teaching us everything we need to know and to be in order to please and glorify Him—including how to be good fathers ourselves.

That's what this next section is about: learning fatherhood from the character of our heavenly Father. First we'll look at God's love and discipline, then we'll look at His jealousy. Finally, we'll close with a picture of the relationship between God the Father and God the Son—the kind of relationship we can hope to have with our own children if by faith we give ourselves to the work of fatherhood.

CHAPTER 4

GOD IS LOVE

> For the earth will be full of the knowledge of the LORD
> As the waters cover the sea.
>
> Isaiah 11:9

IF GOD IS your Father, what sort of Father is He? Of course there are many things we could talk about. Whole books have been written on the character and attributes of God. But as we learn about fatherhood, there are three basic attributes of God I think we should focus on: God's love, God's discipline, and God's jealousy.

Why those three? Well, first, love is the context for our entire relationship with God the Father. God sent His only begotten Son because He loved the world. No love, no Jesus. No Jesus, no redemption. No redemption, no hope. Only Hell. The Gospel starts with God's love. The Gospel is God's love. All of God's actions toward believers are a function of His perfect love for His Son and every last one of those who are hidden in Him.

Then there's discipline. We'll unpack this more later, but in practice God's love for His children looks like discipline. This requires a broad understanding of discipline. It's both corrective and instructive. From His love for us, God is constantly teaching and shaping and guiding and

47

correcting us. Thus some of our most tender experience of God's love takes the form of discipline.

Finally, jealousy. It's important for us to learn of God's jealousy because it must be the frame around which we build our lives and families. If we don't understand our God is a jealous God, we will turn the good work of fatherhood into idolatry. You might be thinking, *Wait, God is jealous? Isn't jealousy bad? And what does that have to do with anything?* Well, more on that when we get there.

We could start almost anywhere, but let's start with love.

GOD IS LOVE

First, God is love.

> The one who does not love does not know God, for God is love. . . .
> We have come to know and have believed the love which God has
> for us. God is love, and the one who abides in love abides in God,
> and God abides in him. (1 Jn 4:8, 16)

Here in God's Word, twice in one chapter we read the unequivocal statement, "God is love."

But saying "God is love" is such a commonplace today. It's a central tenet of liberals that God is love. Those who want to think of themselves as religious or spiritual will even use the love of God to oppose the Gospel, saying wicked things such as, "My god is a loving god. He doesn't need to abuse his son by sending him to die for some mistaken notion of his own honor and justice. That would be divine child abuse. My god isn't hateful. He's loving!"

Christians may be so horrified by such godlessness that we find ourselves wanting not to speak of the love of God at all. But never forget that God is love, and the supreme act of His love was His gift of His only begotten Son crucified on the cross for our sins. "In this is love, not that we loved God, but that He loved us and sent His Son to be the propitiation for our sins" (1 Jn 4:10).

GOD LOVES FIRST

This book is not a Gospel tract. But never forget that your love as a father is based on the love of the Father Almighty. First you must receive the love of your heavenly Father through the shed blood of His Son on the cross, and *then* you can become a loving father, yourself.

Remember, the two greatest commandments are to love God with all our heart, and with all our soul, and with all our mind; and to love our neighbors as we love ourselves.

Note that Jesus does not command us to love ourselves. This is an urban legend. We are commanded to love our neighbors *as* we love ourselves—our self-love is simply taken for granted. (As Pascal put it, even the man who kills himself does it in pursuit of his own happiness.[1])

When we love as fathers, our love must be like the love of God. We are not to wait to love our wife, sons, and daughters until they prove their love for us. If we did this, we would be lying about the character of our heavenly Father. "But God demonstrates His own love toward us, in that while we were yet sinners, Christ died for us" (Rom 5:8).

Don't make your love for your wife and kids conditional on their love for you. Love them like God has loved you, while you were still His enemy.

GOD LOVES TENDERLY

When He deals with His children, our heavenly Father shows His love to be tender. Whenever I think of the tenderness of God's love I recall this description of God's fatherhood toward us:

> Like as a father pitieth his children, so the LORD pitieth them
> that fear him.
> For he knoweth our frame; he remembereth that we are dust.

When the strong man takes into account the weakness of those he loves, dealing with them gently, his is a tender love. When the mother covers the ears of her nursing infant, sheltering him from the booms of the Fourth of July fireworks, her love is tender. When the teenager holds the hand of his younger sister as they cross the busy street, his love is tender. When the husband comforts his wife at the grave of their infant son, his love is tender.

Tenderness is taking into account another's limitations and weaknesses, speaking and acting in such a way as to protect her from dangers and harm.

This is the tenderness the Christian husband is to give to his wife:

> You husbands in the same way, live with your wives in an understanding way, as with someone weaker, since she is a woman; and show her honor as a fellow heir of the grace of life, so that your prayers will not be hindered. (1 Pt 3:7)

Concerning our children, fathers are commanded, "Fathers, do not provoke your children to anger" (Eph 6:4) and "do not exasperate your children, so that they will not lose heart" (Col 3:21). You see the theme?

Fathers are to love their wives and children with tenderness. We are to take into account the weakness of our wives since they are the "weaker vessel" and tend toward "fear."[2] We are to take into account the weakness of our children since, in their relationship with their father, they tend toward anger and losing heart.

So what does it look like?

A tender husband does not make fun of his wife's weaknesses or fears. He doesn't dwell on failures that are the result of her weakness as if each of those failures is the result of a lack of submission or respect for her husband. He doesn't ask her to lift the other side of the refrigerator or crawl under the lawn mower with him. He doesn't ask her to be the one to call and haggle with the cable company over the increase in the bill. He doesn't ask her to picket the abortuary to satisfy his conscience without dirtying his own hands. He doesn't ask her to write the letter to the pastor asking him to shore up the biblical content or applications in his sermons. He doesn't spend all the family's money and demand she work to keep them solvent. He doesn't leave her alone among pagans at the dinner table of the family reunion while he goes to the bedroom and reads a book. He doesn't demand sexual intimacy during that time of month or late in pregnancy.

A tender father does not make fun of his child's ignorance. He doesn't berate his son for not knowing which way to turn the screwdriver. He doesn't demand that his son not cry when he gets hurt badly. He knows the difference between his son disobeying because he's immature and weak and lacks understanding, and his son disobeying because he's rebellious. He helps his son with his homework. He prays for his son when he finds this or that class to be difficult to pass. He plays tennis with his son even though he spends three-quarters of the time chasing the ball outside the fence. He doesn't hassle his daughter about being too heavy or too skinny. When his daughter has no suitors, he doesn't demonstrate fear or alarm.

A tender father lives with his wife and sons and daughters in an understanding way. He tells his wife that if he had ten thousand lives to live, he'd spend every one of them with her—and he means it.

His greatest compliment to his son is not that he's "a chip off the old block," but rather that he's faithful, courageous, and a hard worker. His greatest compliment to his daughter is not that she's tougher and brighter than any boy, but that she's beautiful in appearance and heart, she's cultivated a gentle and quiet spirit that God will not despise, and she will make the perfect wife and mother.

And even though he has five daughters and says this to each of them, he is always telling the truth.

DISCIPLINE WITH TENDERNESS

Let me close this chapter with a story from my own fatherhood.

When one of our children was in kindergarten, we had a parent-teacher conference and were told by his teacher that he had a problem obeying. He attended a Christian school and we both knew the teacher pretty well, so we forged an agreement with her concerning the future. Each day she would send a report home with our son showing whether he had disobeyed her that day; and if so, how many times he had disobeyed. There would be zero tolerance: if he had even one mark on the paper indicating he had disobeyed during the day, he would be spanked.

The next day Mary Lee came to the church office directly from school, bringing our son for his first spanking. His teacher had given him I can't remember how many marks for disobedience, and, reminding him of our warning that morning, I took him over my knee and spanked him. Then I encouraged him to come home tomorrow without any marks at all so he wouldn't have to get a spanking.

The next day, again, Mary Lee came straight to the office with our son and I spanked him.

The next day, again. And the next and the next and the next—for about twenty straight days. The church secretary and the other pastors came to cringe when they saw Mary Lee bringing our son into the office. We believe in private discipline, but after a week or so it was hard to hide what was going on behind the closed door of the conference room. Everyone was rooting for our son to start obeying his teacher carefully enough that she would not put even one mark on his paper.

Then one day his paper had no marks and our son announced to his mother—not to his father who was doing all the hard work, mind you—that he had decided he would give her no spankings as a Mother's Day gift. We stopped getting papers with marks on them.

You think that's the end of the story, but it's not. My point is not the spankings, but something else.

For a couple weeks I prided myself on being a father who had done what was needed to turn his son into an obedient child. I told myself it was fine if my son credited Mother's Day with his change of behavior, but I knew the truth. His teacher, his mother, and I had all worked together, but I had done the manly part of the job by whacking him hard on his bottom each day. Surely this was what God used to change his heart! I had no doubt.

But thinking it through a couple weeks later, I remembered something.

Sometime after the spankings first began, I had been working in the church office and found myself standing next to the wife of an elder who was working at the counter next to the copier. We exchanged pleasantries and then, *sotto voce* and talking to the wall, I heard her say, "I think Taylor needs more time with his daddy." It came out of nowhere and that was all she said.

I looked at her across my left shoulder and she glanced at me, lifting her eyebrows but not saying another word. I was thankful to God for the rebuke of this mother in Israel. Remembering this, I realized this godly rebuke had led me to spend more time with my son.

It hit me that it was only after I had begun talking with and listening to my son, looking into his eyes, sympathizing, and empathizing with him, that he had discovered his newfound obedience.

Now you have the point of this story. Discipline without tenderness is intolerable and will drive your sons and daughters to exasperation, bitterness, sarcasm, cynicism, and despair. You must not do that, and to protect against it you must spend more time with your sons and daughters. More time doesn't mean sitting in front of the computer screen or television with them. It means time listening. It means holding them in your arms and scratching their back and tousling their hair and wrestling with them on the floor. It means taking walks with them and asking them what they're looking forward to—and if it's something you promised you would do with them, it means doing what you promised, and not delaying it.

Our next chapter is about God's fatherly discipline of us. But please! Don't discipline without tender love. The church father John Calvin says the man who doesn't love his wife "is a monster."[3] Certainly we can agree that the man who doesn't talk with and listen to and kiss and hug his sons and daughters is a monster.

CHAPTER 5

GOD DISCIPLINES HIS SONS

God deals with you as with sons; for what son is there whom his
father does not discipline?

Hebrews 12:7

FIRST, our heavenly Father is love.

Second, demonstrating His love, our heavenly Father disciplines His
sons. If we are to be like Him in our fatherhood, we will lovingly discipline our sons, also.

So, father, how do you think of discipline? Is it something you leave
to the wife to do? Is it a nasty duty akin to taking out the trash or cleaning the toilet? As in, "A man's gotta do his duty . . ."

This is precisely the wrong attitude. Until we come to the point that
we think of discipline as a privilege rather than a duty, an act of fatherly
love rather than an act of impatience or irritation, our discipline will
never be of faith. And what is not of faith is sin (Rom 14:23).

Our heavenly Father's discipline always comes from His love.

Those whom the Lord loves He disciplines, and He scourges [whips]
every son whom He receives. It is for discipline that you endure;
God deals with you as with sons; for what son is there whom his father does not discipline? But if you are without discipline, of which

all have become partakers, then you are illegitimate children and not sons. (Heb 12:6–8)

At this point you may be wondering about God's discipline. What are we talking about here? What does God's discipline of His sons look like? I mean, okay, we know it says, "He scourges every son whom He receives," but . . . really? God disciplines us? How?

One day I received an email from a Christian brother who reported an accident he'd had in a parking lot earlier in the week. He'd rear-ended a car and he made a point of telling me that the accident was God's love to him.

Why?

Because when he smashed his front end into the car in front of him, he'd been looking at a good-looking woman other than his wife.

God's discipline looks like that, and it was this brother's faith that caused him to recognize his Father's loving hand in the accident, and to be grateful.

Or take the case of a brother who looked at a good looking woman while she bathed, and giving in to his lust, he took her, slept with her, and got her pregnant. Then, to cover it up, he murdered her husband. Later, when the baby was born, the little one got sick and died. This brother, too, recognized God's loving hand of discipline and was thankful.

God's discipline looks like that, and you can read the whole story in God's Book, 2 Samuel 11:1–12:25. You can also read King David's prayer of confession in Psalm 51.

Many other accounts of God's fatherly discipline are written up in the Bible. In fact, the Bible is filled up to the brim with them. Take, for instance, the church of Corinth.

In this congregation, there were a number of men and women who were eating the Lord's Supper unworthily. So God disciplined them. How?

Therefore whoever eats the bread or drinks the cup of the Lord in an unworthy manner, shall be guilty of the body and the blood of the Lord. But a man must examine himself, and in so doing he is to eat of the bread and drink of the cup. For he who eats and drinks, eats and drinks judgment to himself if he does not judge the body rightly. For this reason many among you are weak and sick, and a number sleep. But if we judged ourselves rightly, we would not be judged. But when we are judged, we are disciplined by the Lord so that we will not be condemned along with the world. (1 Cor 11:27–32)

The Father Almighty disciplined His sons and daughters in the church of Corinth by making many of them weak and sick, and taking the lives of others (those who "sleep" are those who died). After this summary, the Holy Spirit gives such a simple statement of fact: "But when we are judged, we are disciplined by the Lord." Sickness and death were "so that we will not be condemned along with the world."

God's discipline looks like that. It flows from His love for us. He is determined to discipline us toward eternal life.

So now, does this mean every time there's an accident, every time someone gets sick or dies, it's God disciplining that person?

No. It wasn't David's infant son who had committed adultery and murder. It was his father, and the baby died because of his father's sins.[1]

So then, does this mean every time there's an accident or someone gets sick or dies, God's disciplining someone—we just don't necessarily know whom?

No. There are times when neither the man himself nor his parents sinned, but the sickness is for the demonstration of the power of God. You remember the man born blind?

As [Jesus] passed by, He saw a man blind from birth. And His disciples asked Him, "Rabbi, who sinned, this man or his parents, that he would be born blind?" Jesus answered, "It was neither that this man sinned, nor his parents; but it was so that the works of God might be displayed in him." (Jn 9:1–3)

Where does all this leave us?

It leaves modern American Christians throwing their hands up and saying something like this:

"If sometimes accidents, sickness, and death are God's discipline of the person himself, sometimes His discipline of someone else, and sometimes used to show His power, how do we know which is which? And really, isn't it better just to assume the best about everyone and not jump to conclusions? I mean, if we don't know, we don't know, right? God isn't writing Scripture any more and we don't have apostles running around in the church today, so when something bad happens we should just keep our mouths shut and move on quietly. You don't go into hospital rooms and ask the man or woman lying there if he committed adultery or abortion, or if he's been unworthy when he's been taking the Lord's Supper, do you, Pastor?"

Well, since you asked: actually, yes. Not every hospital room, but some. And not always those specific questions, but questions about sin, to be sure. And not just I, but each of our congregation's pastors and elders has done the same.

The Apostle James links confession of sin, prayer for forgiveness, and healing. Following an epidemic in Boston that killed many, the Puritan pastor, Cotton Mather, preached on the warning Jesus gave the crippled man:

> The blessed God pleases to declare that, for such and such ends, he smites with sickness the children of men—at least, those of them he pleases to make his own children. . . . I will tell you what sickness is: 'tis a discipline, under which both God and man expect that you should grow in piety. Or you shall allow me to express it so: sickness is physick [medicine]; 'tis administered for that purpose. Isaiah 27:9, "By this, iniquity is purged, and the fruit is, to take away sin."[2]

SINNERS DESPISE DISCIPLINE

We live in a day when men think discipline is unnecessary, or even evil. After all, *people don't need negative reinforcement. They need positive reinforcement. They need education. They need help making the right choices. They need to learn to love themselves.*

Yes, we live in an undisciplined age. We don't have discipline in our schools. A Christian man who's a French teacher in a local public high school told me if he failed students he'd get in trouble with his principal.

We don't have discipline in our colleges and universities. Recently, the vice rector of a major European research university told me he had a letter from his state's governor outlining a new commitment required of his university by their elected officials. From this point on, fewer students would get bad grades and more students with poor grades and poor scores on their entry examinations would be accepted for matriculation. He was to sign the contract, showing his commitment to policing his university for errant discipline, then return the contract to the governor.

We don't have discipline in our churches, and why bother giving examples? Church discipline is so dead that most people aren't aware it was ever a function of the church in the first place.

And homes? Most children grow up in homes without fathers, but even the fathers who do live with their children refuse to discipline them.

Why?

We don't discipline because we're materialists and think all that matters is life and health. We don't discipline because we don't believe in the immortality of the soul; we don't believe it's appointed unto man once to die, and after that the judgment (Heb 9:27). We don't discipline because we don't think in terms of telling our sons and daughters the truth about God.

GOD'S PURPOSES IN DISCIPLINE

If we are to be faithful to discipline the students in our school and the members of our church; if we are to obey God and love our own sons and daughters by admonishing, rebuking, and, yes, even striking them with the rod; we must reclaim our faith in the sovereign God who governs all things by His wise and holy providence. From His fatherly love He sends suffering, sickness, and death to His sons and daughters "so that we will not be condemned along with the world."

As I wrote earlier, during their child-rearing years my father and mother lost three of their sons to death. There were a number of Christians who looked at Dad and Mud's suffering and asked them how they could continue to believe in the goodness of God.

We children grew up hearing them say two things: first, that they always felt the death of each of their children was more difficult for others than it was for them; and second (and I heard this over and over again from them), they would say, "We were never as sure of the love of God as when we walked away from the fresh grave of one of our children."

When Christians scoff at the biblical doctrine of God's discipline, I always think to myself that these same people never hesitate to say that God has blessed them in this or that. Get it? Every time good things happen to Christians, we are inundated with "Praise the Lord!" and "Isn't He good!" But what about the bad?

Truth is, neither the man whose son dies nor the man whose wife gives birth to a new daughter is arrogant when He attributes these things to the loving hand of his heavenly Father.

Shortly before his death, Dad preached his final sermon at our home church, College Church in Wheaton. The sermon text was Hebrews 12 and the title was "Is Holiness Possible Today? (With a Warning from Esau)." During the sermon, Dad read an excerpt from a letter sent by Dad and Mud's friend Elisabeth Elliot on the occasion of the death of their son Danny:

> My morning reading yesterday fell in Hebrews 12. Verse 10 came with fresh force in the Revised Standard Version: "He disciplines us for our good, that we may share His holiness."
>
> There are times we are tempted to say, "Anything but that, Lord."
> Then He must of necessity say, "Anything but My holiness then."
> Is any price too great to pay if we may share His holiness? From my heart I say, "Even the loss of Jim[3] is not too great, if He will allow me this. But I will have nothing less." So I know you rest too in His will which is forever good and acceptable and perfect.

Dad added:

> It's not easy to undergo discipline. We resist it. Our children resist

it. But it's through the discipline of God that our holiness is molded and that we grow into the men and women . . . who are like God, because God Himself is holy.[4]

Don't worry. We'll come back later in this book to the whats, whys, whens, and hows of an earthly father modeling himself on God and providing discipline to those under his care. For now, we have one more attribute of God to discuss.

CHAPTER 6

GOD IS JEALOUS

> Immediately they left the boat and their father, and followed Him.
>
> Matthew 4:22

FIRST, our heavenly Father is love. Second, He disciplines those He loves. Third, He is jealous.

This sounds wrong. Jealousy is bad and God cannot sin, right?

Yet our God is a jealous God. When Moses was given the Law at Mt. Sinai, God also commanded His people to destroy the idols of the wicked Canaanites and note His reason:

> Watch yourself that you make no covenant with the inhabitants of the land into which you are going, or it will become a snare in your midst. But rather, you are to tear down their altars and smash their sacred pillars and cut down their Asherim—for you shall not worship any other god, for the LORD, whose name is Jealous, is a jealous God. (Ex 34:12–14)

The sons of Israel were to keep apart from the Canaanites and destroy their altars and idols because God's very name is "Jealous." That hits it right on the head, doesn't it? His names are His character. Thus, in the Second Commandment God explains His prohibition of idolatry, saying, "for I, the LORD your God, am a jealous God, visiting the iniquity of the fathers on the children, on the third and the fourth generations of those who hate Me" (Ex 20:5).

You think your wife is jealous for your love? God is infinitely more so. He demands absolute first place in our hearts.

GOD'S JEALOUSY AND OUR FAMILIES

The jealousy of God is a wonderful truth, but why spend time on it in a book on fatherhood?

Because God commands us to put no idol before Him and one of the biggest idols in the Christian church today is the family.

Of course, the Word of God commands husbands to love their wives and wives their husbands; fathers and mothers to love their children and children to love and obey their fathers and mothers; and so on. Still, we are not fully biblical until we face and obey God's command that we never put our wives, husbands, fathers, mothers, sons, or daughters in the place of God.

It's impossible to misunderstand Jesus on this. He put it bluntly and it's as difficult for us to listen to His words today as it was for His disciples two thousand years ago:

> If anyone comes to Me, and does not hate his own father and mother and wife and children and brothers and sisters, yes, and even his own life, he cannot be My disciple. (Lk 14:26)

The Gospel of Matthew gives us a fuller account of this theme in Jesus' teaching:

> For I came to set a man against his father, and a daughter against her mother, and a daughter-in-law against her mother-in-law; and a man's enemies will be the members of his household. He who loves father or mother more than Me is not worthy of Me; and he who loves son or daughter more than Me is not worthy of Me. And he who does not take his cross and follow after Me is not worthy of Me. (10:35–38)

God will not tolerate us putting our sons and daughters above Him in our honor and love.

This leads to constant tension in the Christian father's heart. He is to order his life and everything under his authority to the glory of God. When his own wife, sons, or daughters oppose God, they have made themselves into enemies within his own household. And truth be told, such conflict is much more common than we like to notice.

Even the godly father of a godly family will at various times recognize that Jesus' prophecy is being fulfilled in his own home and he must choose between God and his wife, God and his son, God and his daughter.

Pastors and elders help people through this conflict all the time. The unbelieving husband demands his wife stop joining the people of God in worship each Lord's Day and she comes to an elder and his wife asking what she should do. The believing husband demands his wife and children leave their church with him because he's given himself to pornography, the elders have admonished him, and he hates them for it.

Jesus warned us about these types of situations, not because we'd never run into them, but because they're a constant in the life of His disciples. In this world the Christian never stops being confronted with choices between God and man, particularly his own flesh and blood. Nothing is more heart-wrenching.

Not too long ago in our church, with much sorrow we excommunicated a young college student who had grown up in our congregation. Over the course of several months, this young man had spoken blasphemously to his parents, as well as the pastors, elders, and members of the congregation. He denied the only true God.

After the elders announced his excommunication in Lord's Day worship, I began the sermon by reading the above passage where our Lord forces a choice between Himself and our loved ones. I pointed out that all of us must put God first, above every earthly love and power, and that this young man's parents were putting God first by having removed their blaspheming son from their home and standing in agreement with the elders in the decree of excommunication.

We prayed for the young man and everyone there knew that day was one of the saddest our church had ever experienced. We would all seek the day when this young man might, by the mercy of God, return home, saying with the prodigal son, "Father, I have sinned against heaven and in your sight; I am no longer worthy to be called your son" (Lk 15:21).

FAMILY VALUES?

Among American Christians, "family values" are up there with democracy and free-market capitalism. We believe in marriage, motherhood, apple pie, and children, and much of our support of conservative politicians is tied to our commitment to "conservative family values." Combine our support for family values with our hope in God's covenant promises to our children and you see how we may refuse to allow the elders of our church to discipline our son or daughter who has chosen the idols of the modern Canaanites over God. *But God promised to be the God of my children. I can't turn my back on my own flesh and blood!*

Yet family values start with God the Father Almighty, Maker of heaven and earth, and He is a jealous God who will not share His glory with any other. The first family is not the president's family or our family, but God's family. The first household is not the White House or the pastor's house, but God's household of faith, the church. The first Father is not me or you, but God the Father.

Thus we must teach our sons and daughters that they are to love their heavenly Father with all their heart, mind, and soul. Yes, they are also to love and honor and obey us, but God must always hold first place in their hearts.

As a father you must teach your children that only God is God. You, their beloved father, most certainly are not God. Nor are you ever to displace God in their love, allegiance, and obedience.

How to teach this precious truth?

Well, there's no better way than to confess your own sins to your family and ask their forgiveness. Pop the balloon of your great dignity as their Christian father. Or maybe more to the point, pop the myth your dear wife has inculcated in your children, that Daddy is the best daddy in the world and they should adore him. Bunk, and double bunk!

Jesus put it bluntly: only God is good (Lk 18:19).

Do you see how this reorders today's Christian homes and marriages? To make a Christian home, it's not enough to simply put a man and a woman together—rather than, say, two homosexual men or two lesbian women. It's not enough to stay faithful to your wife and not abandon her for younger flesh. It's not enough to belong to a conservative Christian church and have your children in a Christian school or homeschool them. It's not enough to read the Bible in the morning and do devotions at night. To have your children in a Wednesday night Awana program. It's not enough for your children to know the Westminster Shorter Catechism.

A Christian home is made by a father who teaches his children, "the Lord is our God, the Lord is One, and we must love the Lord our God with all our hearts and with all our souls and with all our might" (Dt 6:4–5).

Our families—our own brothers and sisters, sons and daughters, fathers, mothers, and wives—must never come between us and our heavenly Father. He alone is to have first place in our affections. He alone is to sit on the throne of our heart. He will not tolerate any competition because Jealous is His name.

CHAPTER 7

THIS IS MY BELOVED SON

No one has seen God at any time; the only begotten God who is in the bosom of the Father, He has explained Him.

John 1:18

THERE'S A PICTURE I saw in the farmhouses of my first churches (a yoked parish of two congregations eight miles apart) in Wisconsin's dairy land.

Two farmers have finished chores and are walking from the barn to the house. Each is dressed in bib overalls, each wears the same cap, each has a similar contented look on his face, each strides with visible purpose. They're the spitting image of each other.

But one of the two is struggling to hold on to a large pail he's carrying. He's maybe four years old, so the pail dwarfs him. The work is too hard for him, but you should see his face. Also his father's face. Father and son are sharing work and they're so very proud of each other.

This is heavenly.

Growing up, Dad used to share his work with his children and those were the happiest times in our home. He was a speaker and writer, so when he worked on a book or article or prepared a message, he'd tell us to come on over by his chair and listen to what he'd written so far.

He'd ask us what we thought and it mattered—he almost always took our suggestions.

In a very real sense, then, his work was our work and his glory our glory. When letters appeared in our mailbox, Dad would read them aloud and, whether the reader agreed with the article or not, we took it personally.

I took that privilege of sonship for granted, assuming it was true of other fathers and sons.

It's not. Since then I've realized how rare it is for fathers to share their work with their sons. Mothers and daughters more so—at least in the home—but fathers and sons almost never.

It's true that there aren't many jobs today like farming where it's natural for the family to share their work, but let's not get sidetracked on the benefits of the family farm or agrarian life. My father shared his work with us and he was an itinerant speaker and author, not a farmer.

God made fathers and sons in such a way that the son who loves his father naturally wants to share his father's work. He made fathers to be proud of the son who shares his purpose and calling, who works at his side.

This kind of relationship was so woven through my childhood that I didn't really appreciate it until I reached adulthood and gained a realistic view of other families. How privileged I'd been!

Yet I didn't notice this theme in the Gospels' record of the Father God and His beloved Son, Jesus Christ.

Then, ten years ago, I read this from the Gospel of John once again:

> But [Jesus] answered them, "My Father is working until now, and I Myself am working. . . . Truly, truly, I say to you, the Son can do nothing of Himself, unless it is something He sees the Father doing; for whatever the Father does, these things the Son also does in like manner. For the Father loves the Son, and shows him all things that He Himself is doing." (Jn 5:17, 19–20)

For the first time, it hit me: God was Jesus' Father and Jesus wanted to please His Father.

Jesus loved His Father.

The Father loved His Son.
The Son lived to do His Father's work.
The Father showed the Son His work and the Son was filled with joy to share in it.

So that the world may know that I love the Father, I do exactly as the Father commanded Me. (Jn 14:31)

Now, some of you are probably sitting there thinking, *Uh, what took you so long? Hadn't you read the Gospel of John? Did you escape seminary without learning the doctrine of the Trinity—Father, Son, and Holy Spirit?*
Honestly, I don't know why it took me so long. Certainly it's obvious I had been blind and careless with the Word of God. But, thank God, I finally did see. It hit me hard and I started to read the life of Jesus again, this time looking for evidence of the love of the Father for the Son as well as the loving obedience and honor of the Son for His Father.
And as I read the Gospel of John once more, I found it full of the Father's love for His Son and the Son's submission to His Father.
It was everywhere.
I began to realize how helpful it is as a father to meditate on the relationship between the Father and the Son, and I became convinced that one of the most helpful things for fathers to see and fall in love with is the beauty and glory of the Father and the Son, together. Here is the essence of Fatherhood, and every interaction between the Father and Son in Scripture is like peeling back the veil and peering into high Heaven.
So while thus far we've considered how God relates to us personally—in His love, in His discipline, in His jealousy—I think it will be helpful for us to step back and meditate on this first fatherly relationship. It will provide us with the strength we need as we prepare to move into the practical work before us.

THE FATHER'S LOVE

Culture is the air we breathe that we don't notice, sucking it in from our surroundings, as oblivious to its content as the child nursing at his mother's breast. And it's the culture of Bible-believing churches today to believe that the God of the Old Testament is a brutal God, judging and condemning and burning with fire everyone that goes against His Law. That, whereas the God of the Old Testament is a righteous Judge who won't tolerate anything contrary to His will, the God of the New Testament is a much more likeable God.

We really, really like Jesus, largely because we believe He's more reasonable, more gentle, more gracious, more merciful, and more loving than the God of the Old Testament. As we see it, compared to the New Testament, the Old Testament record of God is deficient in love and devoid of grace. Love and mercy had to wait for Jesus.

Yet as we read the Gospel of John we see that the whole book is a direct contradiction of this type of thinking.

Who is God and what is He like?

For God so loved the world that He gave His only begotten Son, that whoever believes in Him shall not perish, but have eternal life. For God did not send the Son into the world to judge the world, but that the world might be saved through Him. (Jn 3:16–17)

There's no conflict between the Father and the Son. There's only perfect unity. The Gospel of John makes a point of recording that it was the love of God the Father that sent His only begotten Son to die.

Jesus isn't love to God's justice and wrath. Jesus is the fulfillment of His Father's love.

It was the Father who loved the world so much that He gave His only begotten Son. It was the Son who loved His Father so much that He "did not regard equality with God a thing to be grasped, but emptied Himself, [and] taking the form of a bond-servant, . . . He humbled Himself by becoming obedient to the point of death, even death on a cross" (Phil 2:6–7, 8).

When He went to the cross, whom did Jesus obey?

He obeyed His Father. His Father commanded His only begotten and beloved Son to die on the cross and the Son was obedient. Submissive. He obeyed His Father.

Why did His Father command His Son to die?

Because His Father loved His rebellious son, Adam, and all Adam's descendants.

Concerning the love of the Father, Scripture declares, "God our Savior . . . desires all men to be saved and to come to the knowledge of the truth" (1 Tm 2:3, 4).

We must understand that God the Father is not justice to Jesus' love. Consider this unity of the Trinity, particularly the love of the Father for the Son and the obedience the Son gives His Father. Following Jesus' baptism by John the Baptist, we read:

> After being baptized, Jesus came up immediately from the water; and behold, the heavens were opened, and he saw the Spirit of God descending as a dove and lighting on Him, and behold, a voice out of the heavens said, "This is My beloved Son, in whom I am well-pleased."
>
> Then Jesus was led up by the Spirit into the wilderness to be tempted by the devil. (Mt 3:16–4:1)

Submissive Son, proud Father, empowering Holy Spirit: here we see the essential unity between God the Father and God the Son and God the Holy Spirit.

One triune God eternally existing in perfect harmony from eternity past to eternity future. He is perfect holiness and justice and perfect mercy and love—all at the same time. And today, as always, Father, Son, and Holy Spirit work together to accomplish Their single purpose.

As a young boy, Jesus remained behind in the temple discussing His Father's Word with Jewish scholars. Meanwhile, his parents headed back home to Nazareth.

After noticing He had gone missing and looking all over for Him, his father and mother hastened back again to Jerusalem where they "found Him in the temple, sitting in the midst of the teachers, both listening to them and asking them questions" (Lk 2:46).

What kind of an impression was He making there? "All who heard Him were amazed at His understanding and His answers" (v. 47).

At the tender age of twelve, Jesus had a knowledge and understanding of Scripture that amazed the Old Testament scholars of the day—and they were no slouches.

Upset that Jesus had inconvenienced and worried them, blessed Mary said to Him: "Son, why have You treated us this way? Behold, Your father and I have been anxiously looking for You" (v. 48).

Note carefully Jesus' response. Mary referred to Joseph as "Your father," but Jesus replied, "Why is it that you were looking for Me? Did you not know that I had to be in My Father's house?" (v. 49).

This was not the first or last time blessed Mary was corrected by her Son. Here, Jesus made it clear that God was His Father and the temple was His Father's house.

Speaking of His Father's house, one of the more powerful testimonies to the bond of love between the Father and the Son is found on the two separate occasions when Jesus got rid of the thieves who had taken up residence in His Father's house:

> And [Jesus] found in the temple those who were selling oxen and sheep and doves, and the money changers seated at their tables. And He made a scourge of cords, and drove them all out of the temple, with the sheep and the oxen; and He poured out the coins of the money changers and overturned their tables; and to those who were selling the doves He said, "Take these things away; stop making my Father's house a place of business." His disciples remembered that it was written, "Zeal for your house will consume me." (Jn 2:14–17)

Zeal for His Father's house consumed Him.

If you saw a gang of thieves trashing your father's house, you'd fight to remove them, wouldn't you? No hesitation, right? What a man does. What a son does.

It was that simple for Jesus, too. The religious leaders presiding over the temple had turned His Father's house into a "den of thieves," so He cleaned them out. He shouted at them. He rebuked them. He whipped them. He turned over their tables and sent their money flying. He shamed them.

His Father had decreed that His house would be a house of prayer for all nations. Jesus was furious at those who were erecting obstacles to those who would come there to speak to His Father.

What does this tell us about the Father and His Son? Does the Son identify with His Father? Does He take insults against His Father personally?

Along with the scribes and elders, the chief priests mocked Jesus as He hung on the cross. Note the subject of their mockery: "He trusts in God; let God rescue Him now, if He delights in Him; for He said, 'I am the Son of God'" (Mt 27:43).

Yes, Jesus was the Son of God sent to do His Father's work, and at the very moment when the religious leaders mocked Jesus for what they took to be His powerlessness hanging there on the cross, Jesus was accomplishing His crowning work of obedience to His Father. Thus the Apostle John wrote: "We have seen and testify that the Father has sent the Son to be the Savior of the world" (1 Jn 4:14).

The Gospels don't simply record the Son's loving obedience to His Father; they also record the Father's tender love for His obedient Son.

Thus, on the Mount of Transfiguration, Mark records for us: "Then a cloud formed, overshadowing them, and a voice came out of the cloud, 'This is My beloved Son, listen to Him!'" (Mk 9:7).

This is the Father from whom all fatherhood gets its name.

This is the Son from whom all sonship gets its name.

As we turn to the practical details of fatherhood, may we have this picture in our minds and hearts.

PART 3

FATHERHOOD RESTORED

> For this reason I bow my knees before the Father, from whom all fatherhood in heaven and on earth derives its name.
>
> Ephesians 3:14–15

GRAB THE NEAREST BIBLE and read Ephesians 3:14–15. It's unlikely you will find the word "fatherhood" in verse 15, although some Bibles have a footnote giving it as an alternate translation. Most Bible translators today render the Greek *patria* as "family."

Go back to the first English translation of the Bible hand-copied by John Wycliffe and his followers at the end of the fourteenth century, though, and you'll find they translated *patria* "fatherhood." This was correct six centuries ago and it's still correct now. *Patēr* is Greek for "father" and *patria* is the Greek word "fatherhood."

So why does the New International Version relegate "fatherhood" to a footnote?[1]

Today, Bible publishers and their scholars like to avoid some of the words God inspired. And by "avoid" I mean "remove." Given the universal reign of feminism today, it's no surprise the words the scholars have cut out of Scripture are those words God speaks in order to remind us of His own Fatherhood.

Numbers aren't everything, but let me try to demonstrate the fruit of the Fall in our Bible-believing churches today by showing you a count of the occurrences of words such as "father," "fatherhood," "fatherless," etc. in different versions of Scripture:

Year	Translation	# of *father*-words
1611	King James Version	1,720
1973	Revised Standard Version	1,830
1984	New International Version	1,727
1989	New Revised Standard Version	1,185
1996	New Living Translation	1,122
2002	The Message	1,022
2011	New International Version	1,338

Note that, since the 1970s, the new best-selling Bible versions the evangelical church reads contain a quarter to a third fewer occurrences of *father*-words than earlier English Bibles.[2] For instance, the Bible translation most widely used by evangelicals in the English-speaking world is the New International Version, originally issued by Zondervan in 1984. They released a revision in 2011, which they still call the New International Version, but their scholars deleted "father" and its derivatives from the new version 389 times.

In a statement given by the translators and publishers of one of these new versions, the translators and their publisher explain why they've altered the Bible's original Hebrew and Greek:

> The English language changes constantly. An obvious recent change is in the area of gender-inclusive language. This creates problems for modern translators of the ancient biblical text, which was originally written in a male-oriented culture. The translator must respect the nature of the ancient context while also accounting for the concerns of the modern audience. Often the original language itself allows a rendering that is gender-inclusive. . . . There are other occasions where the original language is male-oriented, but not intentionally so.[3]

You see what is going on here. When God's Holy Spirit inspired the Hebrew and Greek words "father," "fathers," and "fatherhood," the scholars and publishers of these new versions tell us the Holy Spirit and the authors He inspired to use those words were limited by the "male-oriented culture" of the times and weren't able to take to heart "the concerns of the modern audience."

So they gagged God.

I've studied this issue for twenty years now and there's only one reason these scholars and their publishers are deleting from the original Hebrew and Greek words inspired by God: we Christians are demanding they give us Bibles that scratch our itching ears. They must account for "the concerns" of their "modern audience."

This is sin. We must stop nullifying the Word of God for the sake of our traditions (Mt 15:6). Until we repent of demanding Bibles that scratch us where we itch, and call for Bibles that are faithful to the Hebrew and Greek words God inspired, Bible publishers will continue to gut God's Word.

They can rip it out of our Bibles, they can try to hide what they've done from us, but they can't rip God's words and truths out of the universe God created.

Fatherhood is everywhere.

SEEING FATHERHOOD EVERYWHERE

Some years back we began a sermon series on the Ten Commandments. Halfway through we came to the Fifth Commandment: "Honor thy father and thy mother: that thy days may be long upon the land which the LORD thy God giveth thee" (Ex 20:12, KJV).

With each commandment, it had been my habit to read the exposition of that commandment by Thomas Watson, a Puritan pastor who lived in the 1600s. His words struck me as a thunderclap:

Father is of different kinds; as the political, the ancient, the spiritual, the domestic, and the natural.

[There is] the political father, the magistrate. He is the father of his country. . . . The Scripture calls kings, "fathers." "Kings shall be thy nursing fathers" (Is 49:23). . . .

There is the grave ancient father, who is venerable for old age. . . . If you see an old man fearing God, whose grace shines brightest when the sun of his life is setting, O honor him as a father, by reverencing and imitating him.

There are spiritual fathers, as pastors and ministers. . . .

There is the domestic father, that is, the master. He is *pater familias*, "the father of the family"; therefore Naaman's servants called their master, "father" (2 Kgs 5:13). The centurion calls his servant, "son" (Mt 8:6). . . .

[There is] the natural father, the father of the flesh. . . .

Children are to show honor to their parents . . .[4]

Sitting there at my desk, worlds exploded as I thought of the implications of such an obvious truth—a truth that had never occurred to me before. They're all fathers—kings, presidents, governors, judges, police officers, mayors, principals, teachers, professors, bosses, elders, pastors, and older men. They're all to be honored as fathers because each has been stamped with the image of the Father Almighty and is exercising authority in His behalf.

Now it seems obvious as I write this thirty years later, but at the time I was shocked to the core by the realization that fatherhood is everywhere. Here is Question 124 of the Westminster Larger Catechism:

QUESTION. Who are meant by *father* and *mother* in the Fifth Commandment?

ANSWER. By *father* and *mother* in the Fifth Commandment, are meant, not only natural parents, but all superiors in age and gifts; and especially such as, by God's ordinance, are over us in place of authority, whether in family, church, or commonwealth.

Female authority is motherhood. And whether in the public realm (the state), the home, or the church, male authority is fatherhood.

Fatherhood is at the great world's core.

When we open our eyes to see God the Father Almighty, Maker of heaven and earth, the scales of our culture's repudiation of fatherhood fall from our eyes and we begin to see fatherhood everywhere, with all the glory and dignity God's own Fatherhood bestows upon it.

Brothers, we are not simply persons. We are not just men. We are fathers, and God has written fatherhood into the DNA of His universe.

Getting this core truth of the universe fixed in our minds and hearts starts when we open our Bibles and see it on every page:

- God is the Father of Adam.
- Adam is the father of the race.
- God names our race *adam* after our father.
- Adam names Eve.
- Adam calls Eve *ishshah* ("woman") because she came from *ish* ("man").
- Adam is responsible for Eve.
- Adam is responsible for the entire race of *adam*.
- God tested our race in our father, Adam.
- Adam alone is responsible for the Fall.

These are just some of the truths of fatherhood we find in the first few chapters of Genesis!

Fatherhood is everywhere, and not because God is a chauvinist. Fatherhood is everywhere, and not because Scripture was written in ancient patriarchal times. Fatherhood is everywhere, and not because when it was written men were the ones who learned how to write and women were stuck home at the hearth birthing babies.

Fatherhood is everywhere because God is the Father Almighty, Maker of heaven and earth, and He created man to testify to His glorious nature.

FATHERHOOD IS AT THE GREAT WORLD'S CORE

I've said it many times now: the healing of fatherhood is the fruit of true Christian faith, and the fruit of true Christian faith is the healing of fatherhood. By the love of God the Father we are restored to loving fellowship with Him as His adopted sons; and from that restoration come other restorations infinitely deep and joyful and healing. We are restored to forgive and love our own fathers; and as godly fathers ourselves, we are restored to loving our own sons and daughters.

We are also freed from the cataracts covering our eyes. Fatherhood is everywhere and we thank God we're finally free to see it and give ourselves to our fatherly work as an act of devotion to God the Father Almighty whose Spirit cries out within us, "Abba! Father!"

Then we begin to recognize the father-hunger that permeates comedians' dark cynicism. We begin to see the father-authority of the robes and the bench and the gavel and the "All rise" in the courtroom. We begin to understand what's wrong with Barney Fife and what's right with Andy Griffith—that Barney is lacking the dignity of his sex and Andy has it in spades. After all, if men were meant to be like Barney, would Barney be as funny?

We begin to "get it." It becomes clear that all responsibility and authority delegated by God to man points back to God's archetypal Fatherhood—not just in the home but also in the church and society. We get it that every man is a father, whether he is single or married, childless or with a quiver-full, just as every woman is a mother whether she is childless or has a houseful of little ones that are the fruit of her womb.

No man can escape the weight of responsibility and authority God placed in his sex. By virtue of his manhood, he is a father and God will judge his stewardship of this dignity intrinsic to his sex. The only question is whether his fatherhood is good or bad, righteous or evil.

Think about this: all responsibility and authority point to the Father from whom all fatherhood gets its name, whether the responsibility is for a nation, a tribe, a village, a clan, a household, the children of a brother who dies of AIDS, a business, a school, a platoon of Marines, a submarine, or a church. God has ordered His creation by spheres of responsibility, and fathers bear that responsibility in such a way that those under them are blessed by their leadership, or cursed. For good or ill, he is their federal head. He is their father and his manhood is not accidental to that responsibility. It's at its very core.

So in this section we'll turn to the three spheres of responsibility and authority in which fathers are called to confess their fatherhood: the home, the city, and the church. How should we serve as fathers in each

of these spheres? We'll begin with a brief discussion of the responsibilities intrinsic to each of these spheres, then we'll move into the practical
application.

CHAPTER 8

FATHERHOOD IN ITS PROPER PLACE

> For there is no authority except from God, and those which exist are
> established by God.
>
> Romans 13:1

AS WE BEGIN to think about the practical applications of fatherhood, it's important for us to start by thinking in terms of the spheres
of authority God has ordained for man. Fatherhood has application in
each of these spheres because responsibility and authority are fatherhood, and fatherhood is responsibility and authority.

So what are these spheres?

The great Dutch theologian and politician Abraham Kuyper defined
the three spheres as the state, the culture, and the church.[1] The spheres
of the state and the church are fairly straightforward, but what Kuyper
referred to as "culture" is not as clear-cut. For Kuyper, culture included business, the arts, the sciences, universities, trade unions, and even
smaller towns and municipalities.

Rather than "spheres," Martin Luther spoke of "estates." And, like
Kuyper, Luther had three: the estate of the church, the estate of the
government (or state), and the estate of the household (which included
all those living under the same roof—servants, apprentices, extended
family members, etc.—and also the workplace). Each of these estates

has its own father exercising authority, with each of those fathers standing under the authority of God.[2]

THE HOUSEHOLD, THE CHURCH, AND THE CITY GATE

For the sake of simplicity, we'll speak of the spheres of the home, the church, and the city gate. Before we move into the specific discussion of fatherhood in the home, church, and public life, we need to understand that each sphere has its proper jurisdiction. Each has its proper place and boundaries.

Fatherhood is attacked today when the boundaries of these God-ordained spheres are violated. God has delegated to the father of a household certain responsibilities, while others He has delegated to the fathers of the church or the fathers of the civil realm. For instance, the instruction, care, and discipline of children properly belong to the father of the household who historically has been referred to as the child's "natural sovereign." Other responsibilities properly belong to the fathers of the church and are not the responsibility of the house father or the civil magistrate.

In each of these spheres the fathers (authorities) are accountable to God, not just for the ways they exercise the authority of their own rightful jurisdictions, but also for the ways they usurp the authority of other fathers' jurisdictions. God is the one who establishes and delegates authority.

Again: "For there is no authority except from God, and those which exist are established by God."

Today, fathers of households must recognize that other people and other authorities are taking care of all sorts of things God has delegated to him as the head of his household. Sadly, many fathers don't even recognize how much weight we ought to be bearing. We don't understand the scope of our responsibility. We take our responsibility lightly, thinking our only duty is to put food on the table and a roof over the heads of our children.

No, our responsibilities for our wife and children, for our households, are much larger than food, clothing, and shelter. We may not abandon those responsibilities God has delegated to us.

After graduating from seminary, I was called to serve a yoked parish of two congregations in the rural dairy land of Wisconsin. When we moved to the small town of Pardeeville, Wisconsin, the Bekin moving van men deposited our furniture and boxes in the parsonage and they were gone. This left my wife, Mary Lee, and me unpacking boxes and setting up house.

It was late Friday afternoon when the moving van left, and I had to preach Sunday morning. Wanting to be ready to study all day Saturday, I decided I needed to take my library over to the church office and unpack the books before I went to bed. This would leave me free to hit the ground running Saturday morning.

There were twenty-three boxes of books, so at 2 a.m. I was still at it carrying boxes of books across the back yard to the church office. Walking back to the house one trip, I found two policemen standing on the stoop shining their flashlights in my kitchen windows. Their squad car sat in the driveway with the engine running. I was grateful they didn't have their siren on.

Surprised, I said hello and asked if something was wrong.

"We got a call that something was going on over here and we're here to check it out," they said.

Identifying myself as the new pastor at the Presbyterian church, I explained that I was moving in and everything was okay.

My explanation didn't satisfy them. They continued to shine their flashlights on me, then inside the windows of the house. Of course, inside the house it was clear that we'd just moved in. Boxes were strewn everywhere and I don't think I looked like a burglar.

Again I explained that I was the new pastor and was moving my books into the pastor's office at the church next door. I even told them I was moving the books late at night so I could get a jump on sermon preparation for Sunday morning worship.

The policemen then explained that they'd had a call that lights were on in the parsonage and it was rather late for lights to be on in the parsonage, wasn't it?

"Yes," I admitted, "but normally I won't be moving boxes in the middle of the night."

"Well, if you ever need to again, it might be good for you to give the police station a call to let us know you'll be up late and nothing's wrong."

For the second or third time I said I didn't think this would happen again, and for the second or third time they said if it did I would want to call the police station to tell them what was going on.

The reader may conclude that Pardeeville was a crime center in Wisconsin's dairy land. It wasn't. The most exciting thing about Pardeeville was its name (pronounced "Partyville")—I had the fun of introducing myself to people from outside our community as the pastor of Our Lady of the Perpetual Good Time in Pardeeville, Wisconsin.

Finally, the policemen left, leaving me depressed. Was this what it would be like to live in a town of fifteen hundred? Was a man's home not his castle? Was there to be no privacy—none at all? Did I have to get used to calling the police station if I wanted to get up and eat ice cream in the middle of the night? What if I needed to get one of the children up to keep him from wetting the bed? Dare I take my son to the bathroom without calling the police to tell them I was about to turn on the bathroom light?

Either the father of the household gets to decide when he's up and unpacking books, or he has to get permission from the policemen. God has appointed spheres of authority.

Shortly after the episode of the policemen wanting to know why I was up so late at night carrying boxes of books, our little hamlet made the front pages of the two newspapers in Madison an hour away. A lawyer who lived in Pardeeville found out from his daughter that lay counselors in our local elementary school were removing students from their classrooms to inquire privately concerning the conditions in their home. Knowing the correlation between the abuse of alcohol, illegal drugs, domestic violence, and children doing poorly academically, our school system had trained these counselors to question the little children, asking them whether they ever saw someone get angry, yell, or hit somebody in their home? Whether their parents got drunk a lot? Whether anyone in their home used illegal drugs?

When the lawyer's daughter reported being asked these questions, the lawyer filed suit against the school system and it hit the front pages of the *Wisconsin State Journal* and the *Capital Times.*

You see the problem, right? Though well-meaning, the school system was usurping the authority of fathers over their sons and daughters, over their households.

What's going on today in these United States is the wholesale transfer of leadership and responsibility from fathers of the home and church to city fathers—to government and its busy bees. This is what Hillary Clinton means when she writes, "It takes a village." This is President Johnson's War on Poverty, today's entitlements, and tomorrow's four-year-old and full-day kindergarten. This is the subtext to President Bush's massive expansion of the authority of Washington DC over all fifty states' schoolchildren called No Child Left Behind. This is the significance of President Obama's nationalized healthcare forcing Christian institutions to pay for abortions. In one fell swoop President Obama transferred authority over one-fifth of our nation's Gross National Product to the federal government (which is to say, to himself).

Keep your eye on the ball.

Hillary Clinton's village is not the home or church. Her village is judges, legislators, social workers, policemen, public school teachers, university professors, and Child Protective Services. And note that, as the authority God delegated to the mediating institutions of the home and church is transferred to the state, there's not the slightest decrease of authority. It's simply moved from fathers and mothers and pastors and elders over to the secularists who are intent on rendering religion childless, and thus building their own naked public square.

So here at the beginning of this section opening up the three basic spheres of authority God has ordained—the family, the city, and the church—let's fix it in our minds that fatherhood is everywhere, and that the boundaries between spheres of authority must be maintained or we descend into anarchy or totalitarianism.

GUARD YOUR HOUSEHOLD AUTHORITY

Which is to say, be jealous over the father-authority God has delegated to you. Yes, if you use pornography in your home and your wife is unable to get you to repent, it's entirely proper for her to go to the elders so they will admonish you. Yes, if a wife commits adultery or abandons her husband, it's entirely proper for the elders of the church to declare her husband's freedom to divorce her. Yes, if a family in the church reports to the elders that there's incest in their home, it's entirely proper for the elders to require the father to report the crime to the civil magistrate and to call that father to submit to the civil magistrate in the investigation and punishment of that crime.

There is always much overlap between spheres of authority and it requires wisdom to know when and how to move from submitting to the father of one sphere to submitting to the fathers of another sphere.

Nevertheless, in our evil day when the civil magistrate is usurping all authority of mediating institutions, we must recognize that it's not those who exercise and submit to proper authority who are most in danger of authoritarianism and dictators, but rather those who refuse to submit to the authority of fathers, husbands, and elders. It is those who deny all authority who are in greatest danger—those who have never seen that fatherhood is everywhere and that it's the good gift of the loving God.

So then, as Christian men, what are we to do with our restored fatherhood in our several relationships and duties? That one question contains about a million smaller ones, and the next chapters will seek to provide the answers. In the next few chapters, we'll delve deeper into how to be a good house father. Then we'll spend a chapter each on how to be a good church father and a good city father.

CHAPTER 9

HOUSE FATHERS: FRUITFULNESS

God blessed them; and God said to them, "Be fruitful and multiply, and fill the earth, and subdue it."

Genesis 1:28

But the LORD was pleased
To crush Him, putting Him to grief;
If He would render Himself as a guilt offering,
He will see His offspring,
He will prolong His days,
And the good pleasure of the LORD will prosper in His hand.

Isaiah 53:10

Take wives and become the fathers of sons and daughters, and take wives for your sons and give your daughters to husbands, that they may bear sons and daughters; and multiply there and do not decrease.

Jeremiah 29:6

TRY TO REMEMBER the last time you heard a sermon on fruitfulness. Most of us would have a hard time thinking of a recent blog post, article, or sermon we've read or listened to on the fruitfulness at the heart of God's providence. In fact, I'm embarrassed to admit fruitfulness was only a late addition to this book.

My brother David and I were talking about the organization of subjects and chapters when it hit us there was nothing about fruitfulness in our outline for this book on fatherhood. Yet God is fruitful and has written fruitfulness into every part of His creation. From birds to apple trees to the marriage bed, the fruitfulness of His creation reflects the fruitfulness of the Godhead. Fatherhood begins with fruitfulness and without fruitfulness there is no fatherhood.

A father is a man who has generated a daughter or a son; or in the case of my father-in-law and mother-in-law, three sons and seven daughters; and in the case of my own father and mother, six sons and one daughter. God's blessing of fruitfulness caused my father-in-law to become a father ten times over and my dad to become a father seven times over. These two couples generated seventeen children, forty-two grandchildren, and (thus far) around one hundred great-grandchildren.

How wonderful that God blesses man with the same capacity for fruitful love that is at the heart of His Godhead!

A DIFFICULT WORK

Of course, not everybody *wants* to be fruitful, do they?

Recently, I've been thinking about the constant excuse mothers give for murdering their unborn children through abortion. They say they didn't want to bring their child into the world only to suffer. Their child would have been unwanted. Their child was diagnosed in the womb with spina bifida or Down syndrome, and they couldn't bear the thought of what life would have been like for him. So they had an abortion.

Back in the mid-eighties, I was at the General Assembly of the mainline Presbyterian Church (USA) to testify against abortion. With other members of the Presbyterians Pro-Life team, I was there to call the denomination to repent of its theological and financial promotion of this great wickedness. A number of us were in a committee meeting of commissioners and were taking turns testifying. The bloodthirsty ones were there to testify also, so one anti-abortion testimony was followed by one pro-abortion testimony, and so on until we had all been heard.

Waiting my turn, I listened to a woman in her late sixties testify in favor of abortion. She said this:

> When I was a young woman, I got pregnant, and, because it was years ago, there was no way I could have had an abortion. Plus, I didn't know I was carrying in my womb a baby boy who would be born deaf. Now, thirty-five years later, my son is a successful artist and he's been able to weather his handicap quite well. But I should have been able to abort him!

I was flabbergasted. I was speechless. I was sick to my stomach. I looked around to see what others were thinking or feeling, but as far as I could tell, the commissioners seemed simply to take this monstrosity in stride. Here was a mother of a successful artist who, by her own testimony, had made a good life for himself despite his handicap, yet she was publicly lamenting the fact that she had not been able to murder him while he was still in her womb.

Tell me, why was this woman angry? Why did she wish she could have killed her son? Was she out of her mind?

I think not.

Rather, I believe that she resented the suffering she had gone through raising a son who was deaf. He was her son and the moment she gave birth to him he owned her in a way nothing else had ever owned her emotionally. This is motherhood and every mother knows it.

This is also fatherhood and every father knows it.

When our children suffer, we suffer. When this woman's son was finally diagnosed as deaf, she began to grieve for him. She noticed when he missed his father's greeting when Dad got home from work. She saw his boredom when he had to sit in church unable to hear the Word of God. She saw the other kids leave him until the end when they chose teams for baseball and basketball. Lying in bed at night thinking how difficult it would be for her son to find a good wife, she cried. And when she thought back on all the times she'd sung lullabies to him while he nursed at her breast, she realized he'd never heard one of them, and she cried some more.

Think of the pain this woman went through in her life, seeing her son suffer, and it becomes clear why she was going to her grave angry she hadn't been able to abort him.

The issue isn't so much the son or daughter's pain as the mother's own pain.

So now, come back to fatherhood and think of the hardship that raising sons and daughters entails. First there's the work of marriage. Then there's the work of supporting your wife and children. Then the work of discipline. The work of love. The work of instruction. The work of leading your sons and daughters to see their sin and hate it, to turn to Jesus in repentance.

Think of the pain of believing God's covenant promises—that He will be a God to us and to our children's children to the thousandth generation—as we watch our sons rebel against God and spend months, years, and sometimes decades slopping pigs in a far land.

Now you're ready to consider why it is that so many couples choose to have dogs rather than children; why so many choose never to marry at all; why so many fathers abandon their wives and children; why divorced dads show up late—or never—for visitations.

Fatherhood is hard, hard work and we're never released from it until death separates us.

Fatherhood is painful. Fatherhood brings us to our knees. Fatherhood is not all joy. It's also a heavy dose of blood, sweat, fears, and tears.

COVENANT FRUITFULNESS

Yet, despite our fears, despite our faithlessness, despite our laziness, God commands us to be fruitful. And no, "command" is not too dramatic of a word.

In the Bible, God commands man five times to be fruitful and multiply. First, in the state of perfection in the Garden of Eden God gives this command to all men across all history: "Be fruitful and multiply, and fill the earth" (Gn 1:28).

Then, after the Fall and the Flood, God repeats this command, emphasizing His desire for numerous children: "As for you, be fruitful and multiply; populate the earth abundantly and multiply in it" (Gn 9:7).

God calls Abraham to become a great nation, and it's not to be through Ishmael, but Isaac. Still, He promises Abraham that his son Ishmael shall be fruitful and multiply also, becoming a great nation (Gn 17:15–22). In the vision at Luz, God commands Jacob to be fruitful and multiply (Gn 35:11). And in the Law of Moses, God tells His people He will make them fruitful, establishing His covenant with them and multiplying them if they heed His instructions and commandments (Dt 6:3; 7:13; 8:1; 30:5, 16).

The theme of fruitfulness is woven throughout God's covenants with man. They command fruitfulness, promise fruitfulness, threaten unfruitfulness, and promise that with repentance will come the restoration of fruitfulness. There isn't a covenant between God and man that does not have fruitfulness at its core.

The Lord God, in warning Israel to keep His law and covenant, promised He would reward their obedience with the blessing of rains "so that the land will yield its produce and the trees of the field will bear their fruit" (Lv 26:4). But not just the land and its plants and trees:

> I will turn toward you and make you fruitful and multiply you, and I will confirm My covenant with you. (v. 9)

And if they rebel against His law and break His covenant?

> Your strength will be spent uselessly, for your land will not yield its produce and the trees of the land will not yield their fruit. (v. 20)

Beyond the barren land, it gets worse: if they continue in rebellion, they will decline in number and bury their children:

> I will let loose among you the beasts of the field, which will bereave you of your children and destroy your cattle and reduce your number so that your roads lie deserted. (v. 22)

Then a horror almost beyond belief:

Further, you will eat the flesh of your sons and the flesh of your daughters you will eat. (v. 29)

When man rebels against the Lord Almighty, Creator of all things, first He causes the womb to be childless, then He causes the children to perish, and then He causes fathers and mothers to eat the flesh of their sons and daughters.

Is this not what is happening across the world today? Fathers and mothers are paying so-called "physicians" to cut their babies to pieces while the little ones are still alive and nestled in their mothers' wombs. Abortion is fathers and mothers consuming the flesh of their own sons and daughters and it's a horror beyond imagination. This is the depth to which God's curse has taken us.

God blesses man through fruit*ful*ness. God curses man through fruit*less*ness.

Which is to say, zero population growth, one-child policies, gender-selective abortion, ECPs, and all the rest of the progressives' agenda for their so-called "liberated women" are not at all what they're sold to be. They are not women exercising their own very personal right to private choices. Rather, each of these tragedies is one more aspect of God's curse of fruitlessness carried out against a wicked people.

At the beginning of Numbers, we have the account of Aaron's two eldest sons disobeying God by refusing to lead worship according to His commands. When they offer "strange fire" before the Lord, God strikes both men dead. Instantly. And awful though that is, the Holy Spirit inspires Moses to add this epigraph concerning another punishment God meted out: "and they had no children." In other words, God's judgment of these men did not end with death, but it continued with His banishment of fruitfulness from them. They remained childless: "But Nadab and Abihu died before the LORD when they offered strange fire before the LORD in the wilderness of Sinai; and they had no children" (Nm 3:4).

Finally, in Numbers 5 I ran across something I'd never noted before. If a husband is jealous of his wife and suspects her of committing adultery, he may take her to the priest and lodge his accusation. The priest then is to test her concerning her guilt. And if the test proves the woman is innocent?

Then the poor humiliated woman will be blessed by the tenderness of God's mercy as He gives her fruitfulness: "But if the woman has not defiled herself and is clean, she will then be free and conceive children" (Nm 5:28).

Go ahead yourself: read through your own Bible and mark every passage that notes God's blessing of fruit*ful*ness and His cursing of fruit*less*ness. It's a never-ending theme of God's dealings with man. If we allow ourselves to think about it, it is amazing that God the Father allows us to share in His fruitfulness by making love to our wives. Why didn't He reserve for Himself the exclusive honor and joy of creating each man and woman? He created Adam and Eve by Himself; why didn't He continue to create every man from dust and ribs down to this very day?

Our Lord Creator could have done it any way He wanted, but He chose to make man male and female and to bless them with fruitfulness, commanding them:

Be fruitful and multiply, and fill the earth, and subdue it; and rule over the fish of the sea and over the birds of the sky and over every living thing that moves on the earth.

This command is still God's blessing to us today. He has poured out on us the ability to make fruitful love; to multiply and fill the earth.

BODY PARTS

Now, are you ready for this?

This blessing of fruitfulness is witnessed to by your body parts. When your wife gave birth to your oldest child, did the doctor or nurse or midwife announce, "It's a person!"?

Not likely.

We must open our eyes to things we're squeamish about—specifically, body parts. God has no body. God is not sexual. Still, male physiology teaches us the nature of God's Fatherhood.

It couldn't be more clear.

Stand naked in front of your mirror and look: fruitfulness is the center of your body.

As Yogi Berra once said, "You can observe a lot just by looking."

In addition to the theology of man's body, we should also teach the theology of woman's body, the glory of motherhood and the origin of every man in woman's fruitfulness.[1]

I mean, does it really need to be said that the fruitfulness of woman's body is not going unnoticed today? Have you too bemoaned the growing visibility of women's breasts everywhere we glance today? And not just women's breasts; our billboards and magazines and news sites on the web are covered with immodest images calling attention to every part of the fruitfulness visible in every woman's body.

So then why so much abortion and contraception and shaming of couples with more than two or three children? If our culture is awash in images of the fruitful parts of women's bodies, why does our culture turn its back on children and childbearing? Why does it reject God's command to be fruitful, to multiply and fill the earth?

God has sculpted the pattern of fruitfulness on the body of every man and woman, commanding us all to be fruitful, multiply, and fill the earth. Do we obey our bodies? Do we obey God's command?

No. We give ourselves to the bondage of lust while repudiating manhood and womanhood, heterosexual marriage, the purity of the marriage bed, and the union of lovemaking and babymaking God ordained to be the fruit of marital intimacy.

We give ourselves to immodesty and lust while rejecting the fruitfulness the objects of our lust were created for.

God gave man the organ to initiate and woman the organ to receive; man the organ to plant the seed and woman the organ to receive and nurture his seed. These things are no cosmic accident. God made man to inseminate and woman to bear the child before and after his birth. Now consider the significance of these simple biological truths.

No one doubts that the children of men are the products of a father's will and desire. The father must take initiative for a child to be born.

And if the father does not want to take initiative, no woman can force him. The same is even more true of God. God's children do not choose Him and make Him their Father. God chooses us so that, having become His sons, we will bear fruit:

> You did not choose Me but I chose you, and appointed you that you would go and bear fruit, and that your fruit would remain, so that whatever you ask of the Father in My name He may give to you. (Jn 15:16)

God also appointed marriage that husband and wife would go and bear fruit, that husband and wife would multiply and fill the earth.

And yet, everything about the birth of children is messy. Procreation is filled with the stuff that makes a germophobe squirm: sweat, exertion, fluids, blood, and semen. But much more than that, there's the messy, difficult, and thankless work of being responsible for a child.

It's not difficult to understand why man longs for sex without fruitfulness. Men today are fine with their sex partners giving birth to bastards. All they ask is that neither the mother nor their child inconvenience them. If the mother wants a child, she can go ahead and have one as long as she deals with the child on her own.

Men today are fine with their sex partners having an abortion. Men today are fine with the practice of Onanism,[2] regardless of whether that practice is under his own control or the control of the woman who is the object of his lust that particular night. Men today want sex without procreation.

Men today want sex that is fruitless and sterile, and thus those twin curses of pornography and masturbation that have rendered the church spiritually and physically impotent these past few decades. Porn is sex without union, sex without intimacy, sex without love, sex without fruitfulness.

Stripping sex of intimacy, porn renders sex fruitless—and that's the point, isn't it?

When a man sits alone, viewing his idols of lust, and he masturbates and spills his seed on the ground, the man rebels against the fruitfulness of God the Father Almighty who has called him to be fruitful, multiply, and fill the earth. Despite his erection, there is no initiative; despite his ejaculation, there is no receptivity, no mingling of flesh, no seed, no union, and no children.

We must turn away from our icons of lust, our narcissism that rejects true intimacy and love, our Onanism that renders our sex fruitless whether we are by ourselves or in bed with our wife.

God the Father commands us to be fruitful, telling us fruitfulness is His blessing on those who live in covenant with Him.

> How blessed is everyone who fears the LORD,
> Who walks in His ways.
> When you shall eat of the fruit of your hands,
> You will be happy and it will be well with you.
> Your wife shall be like a fruitful vine
> Within your house,
> Your children like olive plants
> Around your table.
> Behold, for thus shall the man be blessed
> Who fears the LORD.
> The LORD bless you from Zion,
> And may you see the prosperity of Jerusalem all the days of
>   your life.
> Indeed, may you see your children's children.
> Peace be upon Israel!
> (Ps 128)

God is fruitful. God blesses the righteous with fruitfulness. God curses the wicked with fruitlessness. Which are you?

THERE IS NO SHAME IN CHILDBEARING

So how many children should we have, exactly? Many Americans stop after one or two, voicing concern about world hunger, yet how many of these men and women use the money and time they claim they've saved by their decision to adopt a special needs child, or to become foster parents—or even to feed the starving, for that matter? Choosing not to be fruitful is selfishness. Or, to put it positively, choosing to be fruitful is choosing to share. First, to share your wife with children—that itself is a tough one as every new father will attest. He is no longer the center of his wife's life. Her children are.

But also to share his children with others. With the church and the sinful world. And soon, with his son's wife, his son's in-laws, his son's own children, and on it goes. When a husband and wife choose to have children, they are taking up their cross and following Jesus. He Himself died that He might be fruitful. He gives to all His Father's adopted sons and daughters the gift of eternal life. Christian families who are fruitful are beautiful like their Savior.

Years ago I helped officiate a wedding service in a Mennonite farm community in central Kansas. The bride was the tenth of twelve children. While there, I stayed at the home of another family from their church with eight children. What impressed me about the families I met that weekend was the love I saw between the parents and their children. During the weekend, I heard of a number of children in the church who were fostered or adopted by these large families.

For instance, the bride's father pointed out a young man seated at the dinner table Sunday after church who was married to one of his daughters. He told me this young man had been taken in by one of the church's families when he was a troubled teenager going down the wrong path after his father had died. A godly family opened their home to him and he received their food, discipline, and love. Another family had just taken in two foster children. Is it merely an accident that families with eight and twelve children find room, food, and love enough to take in the castoffs?

Throughout history Christians have acknowledged God's command—"be fruitful and multiply"—to be binding; for millennia bearing children has been viewed not as a matter of preference, but as an act of obedience.

Martin Luther faced cultural pressures against childbirth in the church of his day similar to the pressures we feel in our time. Addressing the problem head on, he rebuked those "who seem to detest giving birth lest the bearing and rearing of children disturb their leisure."[3]

There are circumstances in which contraception is wise. There have been a couple cases when I have counseled members of our congregation to use it. In one case, the mother had a pattern of severe postpartum depression with thoughts of suicide. She had even taken preliminary steps to carry it out. There were several young children in the home and it seemed clear she and her husband should avoid pregnancy.

It is not my point in these pages, though, to deal with exceptions to the rule. Sure, there are all kinds of excuses you can make to get yourself out of obeying God's clear command. Trot those excuses out when your parents or in-laws are visiting, and you'll see how relieved they'll be. Similarly, everyone at church will applaud you for not being irresponsible by continuing to contribute to the unsustainable growth in man's carbon footprint.

Yet the rule (which is to say, God's command) is that we bear fruit. And thus there is never the slightest shame in childbearing. Not in having our first child. Not in having our second, third, fourth, fifth, tenth, or twentieth child. God is seeking a godly seed (Mal 2:15).

Who are we to deny His desire?

YOU'LL NEED HELP

Maybe you're on board with all this. On the other hand, maybe you're having a difficult enough time finding the faith to raise one child, let alone think about having more. If so, trust God and don't lose heart. That's what the rest of this book is all about.

Now you're ready to read one of my favorite quotes:

> There's only one adventurer in the world . . . the father of a family. Even the most desperate adventurers are nothing compared with him.[4]

As we get into the nitty-gritty of fatherhood in the next few chapters, remember this: nothing a man does requires the faith in God and hard work in the face of fear and pain that fatherhood requires. Next to fatherhood, serving as president of the United States or spending the night freezing in Mt. Everest's death zone is child's play.

But faith brings rewards that are inconceivable to the faithless. So it is with fatherhood. Fatherhood's trials and sorrows are far, far outnumbered by fatherhood's blessings and joys.

In the last decade or so of his life, my dad saw the return of two of his prodigal children. I was one of them, and the other has helped me write this book.[5] During those years, despite Dad having his beautiful and godly wife by his side, and despite being sought after for speaking engagements, and despite having a number of books selling well, Dad said to us more than a few times that his greatest joy was his children.

At the time he was saying this, David and I probably scratched our heads and looked at one another cross-eyed, thinking, *Me? You? What on earth is wrong with him?*

Joke—sort of.

But now, together, David and I have ten children and twenty-seven grandchildren, with more on the way. So yes, we have come to know exactly what Dad was saying and how he felt.

What greater joy has there ever been than the Father who, following His Son's baptism, spoke from heaven: "This is My beloved Son, with whom I am well-pleased; listen to Him!" (Mt 17:5).

Remembering the Father Almighty's declaration of approval of His only begotten Son there at the river side, Christian fathers today take joy in beloved sons who walk in faithfulness. This gives their fathers the freedom to age and die with faith that those sons will be used by God to carry on covenant faithfulness to a thousand generations.

Do you find the thought of cooperating with God in raising up faithful children overwhelming? If so, please keep two things in mind:

First, what today is called the "extended family" is a better reflection of biblical households than what we now call the "nuclear family." In other words, when fathers in Scripture are commanded with their wives to "be fruitful," that command was carried out in extended family households. People didn't live on cul-de-sacs with dad, mom, and their 1.9 kids. They lived next to, or with, grandmothers and grandfathers, sons and daughters-in-law, daughters and sons-in-law, aunts and uncles, grandsons and granddaughters, not to mention employees, if they were well-off.

My wife, Mary Lee, spends a good portion of her life painting, cleaning up the kitchen, babysitting, serving as a doula, and playing with her grandchildren in the service of our own and our church's young families. Her daughters and daughters-in-law, along with a number of young mothers of the church, love her because of her constant service. This helps our congregation fulfill the command of God to "be fruitful and multiply." In fact, Mary Lee has an integral role in our extended family's fruitfulness. We don't live with our children and children's children, but we live close enough to serve them and others in our church.

If you and your wife are going to obey God's commands, you need help. Lots of it. And you need to set up your life in such a way that, if your parents are godly and support you in your obedience, they can help. So start thinking in terms of households and extended families rather than the nuclear family (husband, wife, and children).

But what if your parents aren't believers and are actively hostile to your fruitfulness? Or to the biblical discipline of your children?[6]

Certainly such a sad state of affairs makes it much harder for you to live by faith, but there's a second thing for us to keep in mind. God has given us the church for our blessing and help. She is the "Jerusalem from above; she is our mother" (Gal 4:26). The account of the family life of the first church in Jerusalem found in the first chapters of Acts demonstrates that the apostolic church saw itself, and functioned, as one household:

> And all those who had believed were together and had all things in common; and they began selling their property and possessions and were sharing them with all, as anyone might have need. Day by day continuing with one mind in the temple, and breaking bread from house to house, they were taking their meals together with gladness and sincerity of heart, praising God and having favor with all the people. And the Lord was adding to their number day by day those who were being saved. (2:44–47)

> And the congregation of those who believed were of one heart and soul; and not one of them claimed that anything belonging to him was his own, but all things were common property to them. And with great power the apostles were giving testimony to the resurrection of the Lord Jesus, and abundant grace was upon them all. For

there was not a needy person among them, for all who were owners of land or houses would sell them and bring the proceeds of the sales and lay them at the apostles' feet, and they would be distributed to each as any had need. (4:32–35)

God commands us to walk by faith, and He gives us the blessed help of the household of faith. Give yourself to her and be blessed by her service. If you are going to be obediently fruitful, you need support. It's not a necessity to live with extended family members who are supportive of your obedience of faith, but it does help, doesn't it? So find yourself a church that will support you in this hard work.

If necessary, move to be near such a church. Why would we move to a farm with better soil, a city with a good university, or a state where we can make better money, yet not consider moving to be part of a church that would support and help us in the hard work of childbearing and child rearing?

Be creative in taking steps to refuse to be conformed to this loveless and sterile and unfruitful world. Be proactive and surround yourselves with (supportive) family members. Also a church committed to helping you in your life-consuming work. Then, in the end, trust that God Himself will provide you and your family the help you need, and that His loving provision will be above and beyond what you could ever think or ask of Him. He is faithful, and He will do it.

CHAPTER 10

HOUSE FATHERS: DISCIPLINE

His father had never crossed him at any time by asking, "Why have you done so?"

1 Kings 1:6

I'M SURE many of you reading this book have been waiting for me to get to the nitty-gritty. How is a father, a regular old-fashioned father in the home, supposed to do his job? The next three chapters will provide some of the answers. But just to keep you on your toes, I'm going to go in reverse order of the things you'd actually like to think about. So we'll start with discipline, move to instruction, and end with love.

First, discipline.

The word *discipline* is a nasty in the church today and we need to restore it to the dignity God meant it to have. I wrote earlier of our heavenly Father's discipline of us, that "whom the Lord loves He reproves, even as a father corrects the son in whom He delights" (Prv 3:12).

Discipline is a sign of God's love for us, and hence a sign of our love for our sons. Going further, the Holy Spirit teaches us here that the son who is not disciplined by his father is not loved by his father.

In our soft and effeminate culture where every man, including the Christian father, is working hard to be thought well of by his wife and all those predisposed to judge and condemn fathers and fatherhood, you will have to remind yourself of the simple fact stated over and over again in the Word of God, that discipline is love. Repeat it with me, will you?

Discipline is love. To neglect discipline is to be loveless.

When God disciplines us, He is bearing testimony—precious testimony—that we are His sons. We belong to Him and He loves us. Jesus rightly says that we, "being evil, know how to give good gifts to our children." Thus we must give our sons and daughters the good gift of discipline. This is the life of faith.

So how should we discipline?

GOD'S CLEAR COMMAND

There are as many methods as there are fathers and mothers and their children, and that's why Scripture doesn't actually give us methods. There's no prescription, but there are commands and principles.

So let me give one command of Scripture followed by a couple practical words of advice.

First, the command.

We must not refuse to spank our precious children.

Why not?

Because God commands it. Again and again in Proverbs, we read this command. Here are two verses representative of many more:

> He who withholds his rod hates his son,
> But he who loves him disciplines him diligently.
> (13:24)

> Apply your heart to discipline
> And your ears to words of knowledge.
> Do not hold back discipline from the child,
> Although you strike him with the rod, he will not die.
> You shall strike him with the rod
> And rescue his soul from Sheol.
> (23:12–14)[1]

In our postmodern age, it sounds harsh, doesn't it? The whole world—even (and maybe especially) Bible-believing Christians—will tell you God is wrong here. There are many pressures on us today to cave on God's commands. Patronizingly, we explain to Him that we know what He wants, but we have a better way to give it to Him than the one method He has commanded.

So, for instance, we fear Child Protective Services and switch to time-outs and wheedling and cajoling and shame. We argue and reason and whine at our children instead of simply spanking them.

But here's the thing: arguing with our children goes on forever, but a spanking is over and done. In other words, spanking is a clear statement of authority and a timely punishment that, once concluded, is finished and life goes on. Send your daughter to the bedroom and . . . what? She sits up there feeling guilty? Or, more likely, feeling sorry for herself? What good is that? You haven't brought her back to respect for authority and obedience. She's a rebel up in her bedroom and you feel like you've been firm when what's really happened is you've simply removed the eyesore of disrespect and rebellion from the living space of your home. For a time.

Spank her. Don't spare the rod and spoil the child. Don't withhold the rod. "He will not die," says the Father Almighty.

You yourself, obey your Father and do what He's commanded.

This is not to say there's no place for grounding or sending a child to the room or reasoning with your son or daughter. Certainly, yes. Use each of those tools also, as long as you are faithful to use as a critical part of your fatherly discipline the tool of the rod which God has commanded.

Second, when you spank, the whole point of it is physical pain. It seems ridiculous to say, but spankings should never be symbolic. Their purpose is not to express disapproval, although they do that. Their purpose is to cause your son to associate disobedience, disrespect, and rebellion with pain.

Many parents make half-hearted attempts to spank that leave the child unfazed. There are few tears and those that come out seem to be motivated more by the father's displeasure than the physical pain. Yes, of course you want your son or daughter to realize and grieve over your displeasure; but more, you want him to cry because when you spank his bottom, it hurts. So spank him hard enough to make the spanking the thing rather than your displeasure or his embarrassment.

Spanking teaches your son to associate disobedience, disrespect, and rebellion with pain, both in this life and the next. Your spanking is God's providence to your son, writing in his mind and heart the connection God has decreed between sin and suffering both now and eternally. If your son is a believer, don't worry that spanking him will deny the mercy he is promised when he stands before the judgment seat of God. God's mercy to him has been purchased at the terrible cost of Jesus' suffering, and here in this life the pain of his spanking will testify to the work of our Redeemer who bore our punishment for us.

RITUALIZING DISCIPLINE

Whenever possible, ritualize your discipline. Your emotions will always come into play when you discipline your children. In fact, if they don't, there's a problem. You should be enthusiastic to defend your position as a father representing God's authority in your home. But unchecked emotions are also a danger, and the Christian father must be careful to guard against discipline that simply comes from anger or irritation. We don't spank as a selfish act to make us feel better. We spank as a faithful act to make our children obey and respect authority. And really, more the authority of God the Father Almighty than our own authority. One way to set up boundaries and protect yourself from sin is to ritualize your discipline.

Give dignity to your discipline by ritualizing it.

Surround it with carefully prescribed and familiar habits you always follow. Treat it like the order of worship in your church. Spanking should be a ceremony with places set apart for it, words of gathering, words of institution, actions and prayers and kisses and benedictions and departures.

Let me walk you through a typical spanking in our home when our children were growing up.

The first part of the ritual or ceremony was the warning. My wife or I would say to the child, "Joseph, your mother told you that you are not to eat in the living room. Come into the kitchen until you're done with your toast."

If Joseph continued to sit in the living room or only slowly got up and stood a while before obeying, I'd then say: "Joseph, I told you to come into the kitchen. If you don't come into the kitchen immediately, I will spank you."

If he didn't come immediately—and I mean immediately—I would then go take his arm firmly—not violently—and lead him out of the room, back into a bedroom where we would be private. (Except in an emergency, I would never spank my child in public. Give your child the dignity of private discipline.)

In the bedroom, I'd go over and sit down on the bed and hold Joseph at arm's length in front of me with his face looking into mine. He would be expected to stand there and look me directly in my eyes as I said to him, "Now, Joseph, you heard me warn you and you know why I'm spanking you, don't you?"

He'd answer, "Yes." Things were clear. Things were consistent. My warnings were not a lie. What I said I was going to do, I did.

As soon as he'd agreed that he knew why he was getting a spanking, I'd pull him over my knee and spank his bottom hard a number of times that matched the infraction. But no matter how many times I spanked him, each blow really hurt—there was never any doubt about that.

You notice how often I'm reminding you that the point of a spanking is the pain?

Then I'd lift him back up and smile at him and hug him and dry his tears and tell him how very much I loved him and how very much I wanted him to honor his heavenly Father by honoring his father and mother. I'd ask him if he understood and he'd say, "Yes."

Then we'd often—not always—pray. And if we prayed, I'd ask God to give both of us obedient hearts that honor God's authority. Thus, in general terms (after spankings), my children would hear my confession of my own disobedience to God, my own sinfulness, and my own desire for God to change me. It's so important for children to grow up hearing their fathers confess their own sinfulness, and thus coming to understand that God disciplines Daddy just as Daddy disciplines his son. One tragic statement I hear regularly from college students in our church is that they've never heard their Christian father admit particular sins or ask his wife or family to forgive him. I simply cannot fathom how a husband and father can be a faithful Christian without humbling himself before his family by asking for their forgiveness. How do we glorify God before our families if we refuse to humble ourselves?

But back to our ritual of spanking. Following prayer, we'd hug again and smile at each other and return to the living room or kitchen where we'd rejoin the family.

Ritual finished. Ceremony over.

Now a couple comments about that ritual.

First, note there is nothing fickle or impulsive about it. The ritual or habits surrounding spankings discipline the father and mother at the same time as they discipline their child. Just as there's no room for debate or rebellion, there's also no room for responding in anger.

If you or your wife had a harsh father or mother who abused you when you were a child, if you were beaten by him or her, don't make the mistake of thinking you should avoid spanking except in the most extraordinary circumstances. The way to avoid abusing your own child is to spank faithfully, and from an early age.[2] This keeps the child from becoming a monster and the father from having to put up with his monster until it becomes too much and he explodes and beats his son. The percentage of children who were abused who grow up to abuse their own children is one of the tragedies of life, and it happens despite those parents making the most intense promises to themselves that they will never do to their own children what they had done to them. So again, if you want to avoid perpetuating the abuse you suffered at the hands of your father or mother when you were growing up, be diligent now to discipline your own sons and daughters calmly, consistently, and faithfully. And pray that God will protect you from angry hitting, and that He will add His blessing to your obedience to spank.

Second, note how spanking works out to be considerably less painful than other forms of discipline. This was mentioned earlier, but let's get specific.

Which is more painful—physical or emotional suffering?

Honest men will admit physical pain is often much easier to bear. Emotional pain goes on and on and is rarely over. Even the memory of it is painful. Physical pain is more acute for a minute or so, but it's quickly over. So one way to think about spanking's benefits is to consider its mercifully quick ending.

Debates and arguments and whining and threats and banishments to the room rarely bring any catharsis—which is to say, any good resolution and feeling of satisfaction and order restored.

After spankings, though, there is peace and blissful reconciliation. If you haven't experienced this, you're missing out on one of the greatest joys of child rearing. Try it.

Third, reading my description of the almost happy-clappy ritual of spanking and the peace and blissful reconciliation it produced in our home, some might be tempted to accuse me of being engineerish in my discipline. Do this now and that later using these words and requiring those responses, and it will all be good. And if it doesn't end well, it's because you did this later and that now and didn't use these words or require those responses.

I understand your concern. The last thing in the world we're looking for here is assembly line discipline with total quality control. Little men aren't bridges or cars, and their proper discipline, their proper nurture and admonition in the Lord, will never come from implementing a schematic through detailed processes carried out at the proper time as plotted on a Gantt chart. Concerning training, disciplining, instructing, and loving your sons and daughters, don't ever think that it's a matter of getting the equations or code right. Don't think reading this book and following its advice will make your fatherhood smart and your children godly. It won't. Raising sons and daughters requires fathers and mothers, not coders and engineers. Fatherhood is an art—not a science.

The ritual I've recommended you follow when you spank is not meant to be a mold into which you pour yourself and your son, knowing beforehand with certainty what the finished product will be and how it will function. As the years go by, you will learn how different each of your children is and how unpredictable both you and your children are to each other and to everyone else in the home, and this will bring everyone both joy and tears.

So no, my goal in speaking of the ritual of discipline is not to constrain you and your son, but to give both of you great freedom to be the men God made you in all the uniqueness He gave you when He formed you both in His image and likeness. Remember, the Bible doesn't give us methods. The Bible gives us commands and principles, and our job as fathers is to apply those commands with wisdom. When we walk in that freedom, holding fast to God's commands and doing our best to be good fathers by being God's obedient sons, that's when we can expect God to bless our discipline.

Satan is the evil slave master. He will tell you that this kind of discipline is an act of conformity to old, defective norms that will crush and destroy your children. He'll tell you that spanking produces compliant children, conformists, mindless cogs in the machine of American culture. But he lies. And his goal is for you to produce children with no fear of God, no understanding of consequences, and no ability to fight their sin. No ability to say no to their passions and lusts. Conformists. Cogs in his machine. Slaves.

Jesus is the Great Abolitionist. Jesus came to heal fatherhood and sonship so that fathers will be agents of reconciliation and liberation to our sons. The goal of our fatherhood is to work with the Holy Spirit to set our children free. Rebellion always produces greater conformity to the patterns of this evil world whereas obedience produces freedom in Christ.[3]

It's not superficial conformity to spank your son or daughter. It's an act of nonconformity done by faith in the belief that it will be used by God to set your child free. It's not superficial conformity to follow a ritual in your spankings. It's an act of nonconformity done by faith in the belief that it will be used by God to set your fatherhood free. Your son will be freed from rebellion. His father will be freed from irritation and anger. His father will be freed from the bad conscience and neglect of discipline which are the inevitable fruit of losing his temper with his son.

But maybe you're asking why the ritual of spanking I'm describing is so linear, allowing for so little interpersonal dialog? Why not take time to surround the spankings with talk, explaining and applying them in a way that takes into consideration the unique individuality of each child?

Well, for what it's worth, I don't believe in a lot of talk when I'm cleaning a milking parlor or horse stall. As I remove the manure, I don't want someone detailing for me the finer points of bedding horses in sawdust or straw, nor am I hankering after a PowerPoint presentation on the pedigree of the horse that right now is trying to kick me. Just let me get the job done and get out of here—you get the point? Spanking is spanking. The point is the spanking, not the talk. The point is to get in and out of the bedroom, not to try to act as if it's a cozy time when all the deepest secrets of the heart may be discussed and all your desires for deep meaning exchange with your son will be fulfilled. For pity's sake, get it done! Pain stinks. Spanking your child stinks. Being spanked by your dad stinks. So get it over with!

There's plenty of time to reason and teach and love up on your sons and daughters without thinking you have to show your child how very much you love him right before and right after you spank him. He knows you don't want to spank him so shut up about it and get back to the dinner table. Yes, if you wish, pray. And yes, tell him you love him. Briefly and simply. Yes, hug him and tousle his hair. But then, act as if nothing happened and get back to the delicious food that's out there getting cold on your table. The years your son lives in your home will provide you an endless amount of time to study his particular personality and the sins and virtues that go with it, and to pray and talk with him about them. Use those years wisely.

But keep in mind that, to the degree you try to add exhortation, instruction, and deep meaning exchange to spanking, you'll make a mess of them all. Spanking itself is profound instruction, so just be quiet and do that work. A grazed woodlot is neither good woodlot nor good grazing.

Now, the final point about spanking—but really, any discipline.

The father is not through disciplining his son until the order of the home is restored. What do I mean by this?

If, when his father is done spanking his bottom, your son is sulking or stiff-necked, you need to start over and get it right. We're not disciplining for mere external compliance or resignation. Our true goal is to restore the order God has placed in your son's life. He is to honor his father and mother that his days may be prolonged in the land which the Lord his God gives him (Ex 20:12).

So if, after you spank him, your son is compliant but sullen, put him back over your knee and spank him again. Immediately. Tell him that you expect—no, rather that you demand—respect. You demand submission. God commands him to honor you. His stiff-necked response to your discipline is absolutely unacceptable.[4]

Now, about this time, some readers are thinking to themselves that this is a perfect setup for abuse. If a father doesn't stop punishing his child until the child is returned to a soft and respectful heart, where does that leave us with some children who seem incapable of honoring their fathers or mothers? Also, what do we do with some children who, having been left alone in their sullen disrespect for years, may take weeks and months to be restored to cheerful respect and obedience?

Three things. First, Rome wasn't built in a day, and in a home where discipline has been inconsistent or neglected, order won't be restored in a day. Use your head and get a sense of proportion. Then dig in for the long haul and make absolutely certain there is steady observable progress. It may get worse before it gets better, but take the long view and persevere, trusting God to add His grace to your hard work. A well-ordered home should only require a second spanking for a bad attitude once every year or two—not every month or week (let alone every day). If it's an everyday occurrence, go to the pastor, elders, or older women of your church and ask for their help and counsel. Something's wrong.

Second, with some parents and some children, it's necessary to keep tabs on the frustration level and protect the father or mother from getting in a power struggle with the child. There are fathers and mothers who are particularly susceptible to power struggles with their children. They should be aware of their weakness and take the steps necessary to recognize when this is happening and disengage. If you're the sort of temperament and personality that takes things personally, be careful to set up safeguards preventing your discipline from becoming a way to let out your anger or frustration.

This might well mean that you have a commitment with your wife or husband that you won't spank more than twice in any session. If so, fine. Your son's attitude may not have been restored to godliness after the second spanking, but the danger of losing your fatherly dignity and authority is a greater evil than leaving some of the rebellion for later discipline. That's okay.

Third, when you discipline your children, whether the discipline is spanking or a rebuke, never allow yourself to lose your temper. You must never strike your child in anger, whether with a rod, your hand, or your words. This is sin and you need to guard against it. If you do lash out at your child physically or verbally, acknowledge it as sin to your child and everyone in the house who saw or heard it, and ask them all to forgive you. Do it immediately. If you wait, your great pride will convince you that fathers must not admit their sin or ask their children or their wife to forgive them. Once taken, that road is very hard to turn around on.

Father, be faithful to keep a tight rein on your discipline—in both directions. Be vigilant to spank, to use the rod. God has commanded you to use it, and failure to do so is your own rebellion. But also be vigilant not to discipline inconsistently or in anger. God has commanded you not to exasperate your child: "Fathers, do not exasperate your children, so that they will not lose heart" (Col 3:21). Errors of leniency or abuse are equally sinful and must be repented of and changed.

Now, one final word on discipline.

THE SWOOP

Remember that I've said spanking should be ritualized "whenever possible," and I've repeatedly said parents should never strike their children in anger.

There are times when it's not possible to ritualize your discipline. There are times when it can't be private. There are times when your discipline will look as if you're simply lashing out at your child in anger.

In such cases, it's sin to avoid spanking out of fear that your friends, relatives, or dear wife will misunderstand and criticize you. The discipleship pastor of our church explains it this way:

The other day my daughter was playing outside and strayed too close to the street. A car was coming and I wasn't close to her. What did I do? I yelled and I was urgent. She came to me, crying and scared and unaware of the danger she had been in. Was I angry? Hateful? No, I just needed to get her to safety. Were her feelings hurt? Yeah, but it was a very small price to pay. I would jump in front of a car for her a thousand times over.

My daughter is all of two and a half years old. She's not mature enough to understand the love that was behind that warning. It's okay that her feelings were hurt. I was there to hold and comfort her and assure her I wasn't angry.

She'll learn in time.

Let me put it this way: someone once pointed out that foolish consistency is the hobgoblin of little minds. In other words, rules are made to be broken. You and I have a rule that we always ritualize discipline. We give warnings and then give the spankings privately with enough time and space between infraction and punishment to guard against any expression of temper on our part, as well as any perception on the part of those watching that we're simply using our son or daughter as an outlet for our frustrations in life.

Normally, this is good and necessary. But following our ritual of spanking is sometimes foolish, and there are certain times where you'd do well to use what one daughter and son-in-law call "the swoop." As in, swoop in, swoop up the child, and spank his bottom so quickly there can be no doubt what he's being spanked for, and that this behavior will absolutely not be tolerated—not in the smallest degree.

How will your son learn to fear God if you work hard to keep him from fearing you? Watching fathers whose main goal in raising their sons and daughters is to keep his wife and children liking him and thinking he's a nice guy leads me to the conclusion that the father himself doesn't fear God. But what a terrible state to be in—not to fear God.

The Apostle Paul concludes his summary of man's depravity in Romans 3 with the statement, "There is no fear of God before their eyes" (v. 18). We must lead our children out of this damnable state, and a critical step on the path to his salvation is teaching your son to fear his father. Is this worth having your wife irritated at you? Is it worth having your in-laws think you're a meanie? Is it worth being misunderstood?

I hope so.

God's Word records that He doesn't always wait for the Day of Judgment to punish man, and His punishments are as instructive as the words of His prophets. Think of His discipline of King David and David's paramour Bathsheba by taking the life of their son. He was a baby and he died. This was God's discipline of King David (2 Sm 12:15–23).

More, think of God's inbreaking judgment of the whole earth in the Flood (Gn 6–7); of the fire and brimstone he sent on the men of Sodom (Gn 18–19); of the sudden death of godly Abigail's husband, Nabal (1 Sm 25). Then, in the New Testament, we read this of King Herod:

> On an appointed day Herod, having put on his royal apparel, took his seat on the rostrum and began delivering an address to them. The people kept crying out, "The voice of a god and not of a man!" And immediately an angel of the Lord struck him because he did not give God the glory, and he was eaten by worms and died. (Acts 12:21–23)

Wicked Herod got no warning at all. The angel of the Lord swooped down and struck him; he was eaten by worms and died.

But maybe you think this sort of treatment is never meted out to the people of God?

Then consider how God responded when men violated His explicit command by transporting the Ark of the Covenant by an ox cart, and Uzzah reached out his hand to stabilize the Ark when it was in danger of falling. When he touched the Ark, God struck him dead (2 Sm 6:36–37).

But maybe you think this is just the Old Testament and the God of the New Testament is more compassionate? If so, what do you make of Ananias and Sapphira? In the midst of the church, they lied to God, and God swooped in and struck them both dead. After her husband had come to the church and been killed by God for his lie, Sapphira herself arrived. She too lied, and she too fell dead at the apostles' feet (Acts 5:1–10).

Now hear what the Holy Spirit records about the result of this inbreaking judgment by God:

> And great fear came over the whole church, and over all who heard of these things.

At the hands of the apostles many signs and wonders were taking place among the people; and they were all with one accord in Solomon's portico. But none of the rest dared to associate with them; however, the people held them in high esteem. And all the more believers in the Lord, multitudes of men and women, were constantly added to their number. (vv. 11–14)

Do you see how useful inbreaking judgment can be? In the Jerusalem church it produced godly fear that led to repentance and faith. It distinguished between the church and unbelievers such that unbelievers kept away while many others repented and believed.

In 1 Corinthians we read that the failure of believers to discern the body of our Lord in the Lord's Supper led God to judge their sin by making some of them sick and taking the lives of others (11:27–32).

Have I made the point? God Himself swoops down on man and metes out judgment on the wicked and discipline on His covenant people. His sons and daughters. What then does it mean when we do everything we possibly can to keep our children from fearing us—and our wives from being irritated with us? Do we think we have perfected mercy? Are we more fair than God? Can we possibly think that we have perfected the work of child rearing above God's own techniques?

Let me put it bluntly: God swoops, so we should swoop. It is healthy and loving for us to raise our children in such a way that they are never really sure how far they can go into disobedience without experiencing their father pouncing on them. This is the character of our heavenly Father, and it's good and necessary for us to acclimate our sons and daughters to this aspect of His character by demonstrating it in our own discipline of them.

The theme of God's judgment falling upon man is all through the Bible and we avoid it to our peril. God is longsuffering and fathers ought to be like Him in this. But God's patience has an end and fathers should be like Him in this also. Our children must not be raised in a home where their father is fickle or thin-skinned. They must not be raised by a father who is inconsistent in his standards and punishments. They must not be raised by a father who disciplines out of irritation. Must I go on? They must not be raised by a father who disciplines with an eye to his wife's or in-laws' or son's approval. They must not be raised by a father who disciplines out of a fear of appearing weak. Must I go on?

Father, train your sons and daughters to know the character of God. And not the god of psychologists and school counselors and the talking heads of evangelical inspirational radio and family conferences, but the God of the Flood and fire and brimstone, and the deaths of Ananias and Sapphira.

If you love your sons and daughters, you will show them the character of their heavenly Father who thought it helpful and loving to record this in His Word:

> For we know Him who said, "Vengeance is Mine, I will repay." And again, "The Lord will judge His people." It is a terrifying thing to fall into the hands of the living God. (Heb 10:30–31)

In all our work of discipline, we have a choice: we can fear man or we can fear God. We cannot fear both man and God. Either we do this hard, hard work of discipline with our eye on God, relying on His Word and Holy Spirit for everything we need to do the work well, or we do it with our eye on our wife, seeking her approval or the approval of the child himself. But in the discipline of our children, as in everything else, we cannot love this world and love God. We must choose, and I exhort you to love God and do as He commands. Discipline your son. Use the rod. Spank him. You will not lose his friendship. Your marriage will not end.

As I'm writing this, all the protests and questions and challenges running through your mind right now are coming to me. *But . . . But!*

Look, this is a book on fatherhood, so we can't turn it into a book on discipline. But as you work towards faithfulness in discipline, keep a few things in mind.

First, as a father, this is your greatest work and you will die surrounded by its fruit, good or bad. You will do the hard work of instruction, training, and discipline, and die surrounded by godly children, spouses, and grandchildren; or you will neglect your duties and die surrounded by covenant breakers. Now don't get wrapped up in the exception that proves the rule. Sure, in some of our homes there are Esaus whose rebellion is not because of, but in spite of, our faithful discipline. But right now I'm not talking about them. Do the work of discipline that will allow you to die in peace.

Second, when God is specific in His commands, He expects your obedience to be as specific as His command. As we have seen, He doesn't simply shower us with nostrums about raising self-confident children who are passionate in their pursuit of excellence. He commands us:

> Do not hold back discipline from the child,
> Although you strike him with the rod, he will not die.
> You shall strike him with the rod
> And rescue his soul from Sheol.

If your main concern is to avoid your wife's disapproval, you will disobey this command of God. It's that simple. So whose approval do you want? Whom do you trust? What fruit are you seeking?

If you think you can raise up godly children while avoiding the use of the rod, you are a rebel against God. Don't think that you know where God's heading but you have a better way to get there. Every foolish father tells himself that. Every foolish Christian, also.

Don't ever forget that God appoints both ends and means, both goals and methods of getting to those goals. "Do not hold back discipline," and "strike him with the rod."

Third, speaking of love . . .

When you gain the faith to work hard at disciplining your children and you begin to relish that work and its obvious wonderful fruit, you'll see that this is your true love for your sons and daughters. The whole godless world prattles on about love but knows nothing of it. Meanwhile, the acts that Christians do by faith (the very acts condemned by the world as "unloving") are the proofs of our love. Or rather, they *are* our love. Remember Hebrews tells us, "those whom the Lord loves He disciplines" (12:6; Prv 3:12). Remember that God is the Father from whom all fatherhood in heaven and earth gets its name.

Should we not take responsibility for our sons as our heavenly Father does for His sons?

CHAPTER 11

HOUSE FATHERS: INSTRUCTION

These words, which I am commanding you today, shall be on your heart. You shall teach them diligently to your sons and shall talk of them when you sit in your house and when you walk by the way and when you lie down and when you rise up. You shall bind them as a sign on your hand and they shall be as frontals on your forehead. You shall write them on the doorposts of your house and on your gates.

Deuteronomy 6:6–9

Go, inquire of the LORD for me and the people and all Judah concerning the words of this book that has been found, for great is the wrath of the LORD that burns against us, because our fathers have not listened to the words of this book, to do according to all that is written concerning us.

2 Kings 22:13

A father tells his sons about Your faithfulness.

Isaiah 38:19

FOR GOOD OR ILL, the father's instruction has more influence on his children than the influence or instruction of anyone else. Like it or not, as the acorn never falls far from the tree, sons and daughters never fall far from their father.

WHAT'S AT STAKE

For instance, when they become adults, sons and daughters' commitment to church follows their father much more than their mother. Adults are most likely to worship God if they grew up in a home where their father and mother attended worship themselves, and took their children with them. But if only one of their parents went to church, it very much matters which parent it was. Most children *will not* attend church as adults if they grew up attending worship with just their mother, but they *will* attend church if they grew up attending worship with just their father.[1]

From the womb, children are one with their mothers. They love them and learn most everything they need to know from them, first at their breast, then at their knee, then toddling after them with their blankie. The majority of a child's learning is already accomplished long before mom and dad decide whether their child will be homeschooled, Christian schooled, or public schooled.

Still, God has placed responsibility on the children's father, and this is evident in the depth of leadership and influence every father has with his children—even (and maybe especially) in a home where the children are raised by the best mother in the world.

Now some fathers think they ought to avoid meddling with their sons and daughters' natural inclinations. After all, religious or spiritual matters are deeply personal things. Priding himself on how hands-off he is, a father will say to me, "I don't force my son to go to church. I want him to make up his own mind about religion."

Of course it is absurd to think any true Christian would say such a thing. Why?

In both the Old and New Testaments, God's promises are familial, from father to son to son. He promises fathers who have placed their faith in Him that they will have lots of descendants—children, grandchildren, great-grandchildren—and that His covenant blessings will run down through those descendants from generation to generation. Then He tells the godly father how those blessings will be passed down, and His method has always been godly fathers disciplining and teaching their children.

Here is what God charged the fathers of Israel concerning their sons:

> Now this is the commandment, the statutes and the judgments which the LORD your God has commanded me to teach you, that you might do them in the land where you are going over to possess it, so that you and your son and your grandson might fear the LORD your God, to keep all His statutes and His commandments which I command you, all the days of your life, and that your days may be prolonged. (Dt 6:1–2)

Look at what rests on the shoulders of the father. If he doesn't obey these things, his children won't obey God—start with that. But there's more: when a father doesn't himself learn, obey, and pass on to his son the ways of God, his son's life will not be prolonged. Which is to say, his son will die young.

Every pastor can tell you of the little boy who grew up alongside a father who was a rebel against God and who refused to teach and discipline his own son, and how that son grew up to be a young man who had no fear of God and died young. True to His Word, God did not prolong his days. And you know what? At the funerals of these sons, such a father doesn't take responsibility for his son's early death. If he refused to take responsibility for his son's instruction and discipline in life, why would he take responsibility when his son dies? Quite the opposite, often such a father refuses to mourn his son's death, acting as if dying young is glorious: "He went out doing what he loved best." "He lived more in his twenty-five years than most men who live to be eighty." As if his son's early death is no judgment, but a choice.

So now, step back, take a deep breath, and look carefully at all that is at stake with your fatherly instruction of your children. Their obedience of God. Their fear of God. The length of their lives.

If you teach your children the commandments, statutes, and judgments of the Lord, what wonderful promises you have been given. Regardless of how bad he is at the piano, how many tryouts for the travel soccer club he fails, how crooked his teeth are, how many pimples he has, what an old beater his best friend drives—why, even if your dear son chooses to be a painter instead of going to college (and no, not an artiste painter, but just a regular ol' painter-painter)—your precious son will obey and fear the Lord, and the Lord will prolong his life.

Every last power in this evil world will work to convince you it's the other way around—that the good life is money, skill, good looks, a good marriage, and the right college—but it's all a grand lie.

You know how your wife worries herself sick about the education and curriculum choices she's made for her children? It seems as if their very lives are at stake, doesn't it? This is how God made woman. (It's the reason women make such good employees. They approach every task with the intensity and jealousy of a mother hovering over her brood of children.) So don't fault her for what comes naturally. This is an aspect of femininity that is mostly helpful to children, but only if the father is wise enough to be obstructionist where and when it matters.

And one place it matters a great deal is in the education of our children.

FATHERS AND EDUCATION

What are the godly father's priorities concerning the education of his sons and daughters? And note I didn't write, "his wife's children"; if you think that way, you'll please your wife and squander your children. Consider them your sons and daughters, first and foremost, because God has made you head of your home. Concerning the wellbeing of your children, the buck stops with you. So again, what are the godly father's priorities concerning the education of his sons and daughters?

A few verses after this warning of the consequences of fathers not passing on to their sons "the commandment, the statutes and the judgments" of the Lord, Moses commands fathers to redeem the time. They are to take every occasion as an opportunity to further the biblical education of their sons:

These words, which I am commanding you today, shall be on your heart. You shall teach them diligently to your sons and shall talk of them when you sit in your house and when you walk by the way and when you lie down and when you rise up. You shall bind them as a sign on your hand and they shall be as frontals on your forehead. You shall write them on the doorposts of your house and on your gates. (Dt 6:6–9)

Let's talk a bit about priorities. There's only so much time in life and your years with your children will soon be over. Even fathers and mothers of large families will live most of their lives without children in their homes. The years of child rearing are quickly over, so how do you redeem the time?

Priorities, priorities. You have received God's command to teach His words to your children diligently. You're to be a harp of ten thousand strings that harps on one string relentlessly, and that string is the Word of God.

You may think you can trust other Christians, and particularly your wife, to have the same priority you've been given by God, but you can't. You have to fight for the right priority in the raising and training and education and discipline of your children, and your battle is not simply with the world. There will be times when you must also fight the church and your children's precious mother. The Word and words of God are to be preeminent among all the good things clamoring for the minds and hearts and hours of your home and your children. So put on your mud boots, roll up your sleeves, and dig in.

Remember the story of Jesus visiting Mary and Martha?

Jesus was teaching and it irritated Martha that Mary was sitting listening to Him when she was needed in the kitchen. Martha went to Jesus and asked him to remind her sister of her proper priorities.

But the Lord answered and said to her, "Martha, Martha, you are worried and bothered about so many things; but only one thing is necessary, for Mary has chosen the good part, which shall not be taken away from her." (Lk 10:39–42)

How many things are necessary?

One.

What is that one thing?

Sitting at the Lord's feet, listening to His Word.

Fathers are to govern their home by Scripture because:

All Scripture is inspired by God [literally, "God-breathed"] and profitable for teaching, for reproof, for correction, for training in righteousness; so that the man of God may be adequate, equipped for every good work. (2 Tm 3:16–17)

Every word of the Bible is the Word of our Lord. Thus the one thing necessary is for us and our children to be devoted to the Word of God. This begins by our faithfully attending the preaching and teaching of Scripture by the officers of Christ's church. It continues by our taking every step possible to make His Word the very center of our family life.

And yes, it is still true today as it was true in the time of our Lord Jesus that doing dishes and cutting the grass and doing homework and cleaning the bathroom and cooking and doing the laundry and practicing the piano and writing papers get in the way of that one thing necessary.

Let me give you an example.

About fifteen years ago, a dear brother in our church called and said he had just decided he was going back to Germany to serve as a missionary. What's the backstory?

This brother had grown up as a missionary kid in Austria. His father and mother had spent their lives as church planters there, and when their son went into high school, they sent him off to study at a well-known missionary boarding school. It had been a tough time; he felt very lonely and missed his father and mother a great deal.

Ten or so years later, he had graduated from high school, had received his BA from a Christian liberal arts college, and was just completing his course work for a PhD in English literature at Indiana University. He was a member of our congregation and growing in godliness and leadership. He had been an invaluable servant of the church during the four years I'd known him.

Then came the day he called to say he was going out as a missionary.

His announcement came out of the blue. He'd been on the fast track to complete his PhD and I knew his plans were to take a few years to complete his dissertation and then get a job at a Christian liberal arts college.

But then everything changed.

On the phone he explained he was calling from the laundromat. While waiting for his clothes to dry, he'd been reading the Luke 10 account of Mary and Martha when the words "only one thing is necessary" hit him hard. Immediately he knew the one thing necessary for him was not completing his course work and writing his dissertation, but returning to Germany and serving as a housefather to the other young men in the dorm who were as lonely and in need of a father as he had been years earlier.

So immediately he called and said he was leaving Indiana University and returning to Black Forest Academy. It was clear to him that God had just called him to be a father to the fatherless. It was the one thing necessary and he would do it.

You do see how almost anyone who knew and loved him would have sought to bring him back to his better mind, don't you?

What on earth?! You're doing what? Immediately? You can't be serious. Pick up and leave when all that stands between you and your doctorate are a few courses and writing your dissertation? Why don't you wait two years and leave with your PhD in hand? What kind of stewardship of the last four years is it to leave in the middle of your work? It's very irresponsible. Impetuous. Ill-advised. Did you get good counsel before you made your decision? Whom did you talk to? How long have you been praying about this?

By God's grace, the elders did not seek to dissuade their brother, but called on the congregation to join them in sending him off to serve as a housefather at Black Forest Academy. He was our congregation's first missionary, and, over the course of the next few years, we took joy in his reports from Germany. He wrote once saying that he loved his work; that he held Bible studies, catechized his young men using the Westminster Shorter Catechism, ate with them, and even did their laundry—I particularly remember that part.

Five or so years later, he returned to Indiana University to complete his PhD. He'd been granted a leave of absence and so it was just a formality to reenter the program. But having reentered, he ran into a brick wall. His major professor had left Indiana University during his time away and no other prof was willing to oversee his completion of the degree.

He came in to talk and I asked several questions. Had he made enemies in the department? Had his course work been good? Could I see his transcript for the course work he'd completed?

He brought in his transcript and I saw his course work was not the problem. He'd gotten straight As.

We discussed appealing his situation to a dean. It seemed like he would have a good chance of getting help from the administration, but it would make a stink.

Considering the possibility, my friend decided against appealing his situation. He didn't want to cause a ruckus, so he left grad school and took a position teaching English at a Bible college where the president knew him and was eager for him to join the faculty.

Of course, this position didn't give him the prestige teaching at colleges like Calvin or Gordon or Westmont would have. So again, when he gave himself to the one thing necessary, was he impetuous? Wasteful? Wrong?

It's now ten years later and my friend is married with three children on earth and another in Heaven. He's still teaching at the Bible college (although they don't call themselves that any more) and he still doesn't have his PhD. It's hard to complete a dissertation, teach literature and composition, be a loving husband, a faithful father, and a wise and helpful elder, all at the same time. And he had the added burden of having to do additional course work at the university nearby because their requirements differed from those of Indiana University. Still, he's All But Dissertation, well loved by his wife and children, as well as the students and faculty of his school and the souls of his congregation, and nearing the end of his dissertation.

Finally, then: was he wrong? Unwise? Too spiritual?

Peter began to say to Him, "Behold, we have left everything and followed You." Jesus said, "Truly I say to you, there is no one who has left house or brothers or sisters or mother or father or children or farms, for My sake and for the gospel's sake, but that he will receive a hundred times as much now in the present age, houses and brothers and sisters and mothers and children and farms, along with persecutions; and in the age to come, eternal life. But many who are first will be last, and the last, first." (Mk 10:28–31)

Fathers, it is your work to protect your home from the practical-mindedness and efficiency of your precious wife when, like Martha, she obstructs the one thing necessary for your marriage and children and household to be fruitful for God. She means well. You married her for her intellectual gifts and administrative abilities and sober-mindedness and frugality (although her beauty and sweetness and modesty and femininity were not an inconsiderable part of her attractiveness, either).

You have been blessed by her schedules, by her loving prodding about how you spend money and why you're so often late for dinner. Almost everything about this prudent wife God gave you is a blessing beyond your wildest dreams, yet sometimes you have to admit she gets between you and the children when you are trying to lead your household into greater faith, greater submission to God, greater sacrifice for the Kingdom of Heaven, growth in hospitality, and changed priorities putting some specific commands of Scripture back at the center of your home.

But what did Jesus say—how many things are necessary?

One thing.

And what is that one thing?

The Word and words of God—that's the one thing absolutely necessary.

God has made your wife an efficiency machine able to juggle twenty batons or thirty balls at a time, but you are the father of her children and you're useless to her if you don't reorder her priorities in order to protect the pride of position of the one thing necessary. Don't fail your children. Don't fail your wife. Guard your home from Martha's attempt to change her home's priorities. Exercise your authority.

G. K. Chesterton points out that "education is tradition," and where men claim to be educating without authority, they're doing nothing of the sort. After listing the names of several men who might be said to have been educators or teachers in his own day, Chesterton wrote:

The only thing they share is the one thing they profess to dislike: the general idea of authority. It is quaint that people talk of separating dogma from education. Dogma is actually the only thing that cannot be separated from education. It *is* education. A teacher who is not dogmatic is simply a teacher who is not teaching.[2]

Now, father, get your mind around these truths, because Chesterton is simply reiterating what Scripture repeatedly demands of us. Like the pastor and elder, it's the father's duty simply to pass on to his sons and daughters the Christian tradition. He is commanded to command his sons and daughters to "keep the way of the Lord." To "keep" it. To maintain it. To preserve it.

CHAPTER 12

HOUSE FATHERS: LOVE

Above all, keep fervent in your love for one another, because love covers a multitude of sins.

1 Peter 4:8

THIS IS THE final chapter on house fathers and we need to end with love. Why?

Because "love covers a multitude of sins," and fathers sin. Christian fathers sin. John, the apostle of love, calls us out:

If we say that we have no sin, we are deceiving ourselves and the truth is not in us. If we confess our sins, He is faithful and righteous to forgive us our sins and to cleanse us from all unrighteousness. If we say that we have not sinned, we make Him a liar and His word is not in us. (1 Jn 1:8–10)

LEAD IN LOVE

One day Mary Lee came up to the bedroom where I was working and asked me to come downstairs and deal with one of our daughters. Four or so years old, this daughter had been playing with a neighbor-friend and had been sent home. When she came in the house, Mary Lee had asked her why she was sent home and our daughter responded, "I don't know." Her mother persisted several times, questioning what had happened, but our daughter denied knowing anything about why she had been sent home.

At this point Mary Lee concluded that our daughter was holding out on her; that she knew why she had been sent home but didn't want to admit what she had done. So Mary Lee came to me and asked me to take over.

I took our daughter into our guest bedroom downstairs and, sitting down on the bed, I had her stand in front of me and asked her, "Why were you sent home?"

My daughter responded, "I don't know, Daddy."

I repeated my question: "Hannah, why were you sent home?" And she repeated her response: "I don't know why, Daddy."

Now you must understand that Hannah was rarely a disciplinary problem. This was out of character for her, so both her mother and I were concerned that we had begun a new era in Hannah's character and development when she would be stubborn and lie. So I persisted in my questioning, saying to her, "Hannah, if you don't tell me why you were sent home, Daddy will spank you. Do you understand?"

She said yes, she understood, so then I repeated my question: "Why were you sent home?"

Hannah again responded, "I don't know, Daddy."

Yes, I spanked her. It seemed clear she was holding out on us and it could not be tolerated. If we asked her a question, she must answer— and answer truthfully.

After spanking her, I again asked the question: "Why were you sent home?"

Again, she repeated the answer she had given her mother and me ten times or so already: "I don't know, Daddy."

Probing for something, anything, I said, "Did you do something wrong?"

She responded, "I don't think so."

So, again, I warned that I would spank her unless she told me why she had been sent home, asking her, "Why were you sent home?"

She answered, "I don't know, Daddy."

I despaired at the change I was seeing in my precious child. You know the feeling. Inside I felt scared, but once more I turned her over my knee and spanked her.

Of course I hugged and kissed her, loving on her as I disciplined my precious daughter. But Mary Lee had asked me to get at the truth and I was determined to do so. So again, I asked her, "Hannah, listen to me! You MUST tell me what you did. Why were you sent home? Did you say something bad? Did you call your friend a bad name?"

This time there was a variation in Hannah's response as she answered, "Maybe, Daddy."

I said, "Maybe? What did you call her?"

Hannah answered haltingly, "A chest of drawers?" And yes, that's how she said it. It was more a question than an answer.

Suddenly, I saw the whole thing clearly—starting with the chest of drawers. As she had said "chest of drawers," she had been looking across the bedroom at a chest of drawers. She was doing what any obedient little girl would do when her father was searching for something: she was trying to help him find it and she wondered whether "a chest of drawers" might be what he was looking for. I was sickened. I had repeatedly questioned her, not believing her multiple repetitions of "I don't know, Daddy." I had spanked her twice and she had been unable to obey me because . . .

Because she had not been sent home for doing anything wrong at all, nor had she said anything bad, nor had she called her playmate any names. I called Mary Lee and told her that I didn't think Hannah had said or done anything wrong. I asked Mary Lee to call Hannah's playmate's mother and ask her what had happened. Mary Lee did so and quickly returned to report that the playmate's mother had said her daughter was being manipulative with Hannah, so she (the mother) had sent Hannah home as a way of disciplining her own daughter.

Why such a long story?

Because it illustrates the brokenness of family life and fatherhood. Also, because, to this day, we tell this story among our adult children and their own little ones and we laugh and laugh and laugh.

Why?

Not because we're making light of Hannah's suffering. As I write, I'm almost in tears remembering that afternoon. How I wish I could take it back.

And yet, all fathers sin and we must make sure our homes are permeated with love so that it covers our sins as well as the sins of our wife and children.

This is true of all spiritual work: if we wait to obey God and serve others until our service is perfect, we'll never do our work, which means we'll never give our gifts to the household of faith. When any pastor walks to the pulpit or the Lord's Table, he is deeply aware of his own failures to serve God as he ought, to obey as he should, to love as he is commanded. Yet he has a job to do and he must not abdicate his responsibilities because of his many failures.

If we love them, our families will follow us in our failures. Together, love will cover the family's multitude of sins, including Daddy's sins. The loving father has a loving household. Do your children wait until you count to ten to obey? It's because you have taught them not to obey until you count to ten. Do your children eat like slobs? It's because you have taught them to eat like slobs. Do your sons and daughters love one another? It's because you have taught them to love one another.

They don't love one another because you have yelled at them when they fight or because you have had them memorize 1 Corinthians 13 (although, of course, you should discipline them when they fight with each other and it would certainly be good to have each of your children memorize 1 Corinthians 13). They love one another because you first loved their mother and each of them.

We've repeatedly pointed out that discipline is love, and the father who doesn't discipline his children doesn't love them. We've also shown that the father who instructs or teaches his children is loving them. But now we turn to the tender side of fatherhood that is most commonly thought of as love. The Apostle Paul gives us this command:

Be kind to one another, tender-hearted, forgiving each other, just as God in Christ also has forgiven you. (Eph 4:32)

Love is kind and tender-hearted and it produces the bond of forgiveness that holds families together through the challenges we face each day as we sin and sin and sin against one another.

Without love, what happens?

> The whole Law is fulfilled in one word, in the statement, "You shall love your neighbor as yourself." But if you bite and devour one another, take care that you are not consumed by one another. (Gal 5:14–15)

Without love, we bite and devour one another, we consume one another. My dad once wrote that a sure way of telling the condition of a church's family life, its fellowship, was to go into the church's kitchen and run a hand over the top of the plates in the cabinets. If they have dust on them, there's a good chance the church is biting and devouring one another.

It's similar with your home. If you don't eat together, it's likely your home has a tone of hostility—or worse, indifference. But if you eat together, you are making daily investments in tenderness, kindness, good manners, putting others before yourself; and then, joyful unity prevails. So the first thing fathers should do to cultivate their love for their wife and children is to set up the home and its work and schedules so the family is able to eat together. The common table produces a common heart.

Yes, there will be many challenges to be faced, but once again, it is your job as the father of the home to set your home's priorities. Don't let yourself off the hook by allowing your work to keep you out in the barn, inside your office, or driving your truck until late in the evening. Go into the house and eat with your family. Go home and walk into the house with open arms, kissing your wife first, then hugging each of your children. Bless your household with your tender love. Make it a daily routine, and then be sure to keep it from decaying into *merely* a daily routine. Smell the food and smile. Taste the soup and compliment your wife. If you can do it without fighting, help with the cooking. And if you can't help her with the cooking without showing how hangry you are, after the meal is over clean up the kitchen.

Yes, there will be many challenges to be faced if you set out to have a family dinner each day, but persevere. Do what is necessary to make your family one loving mass of humanity who eats and reads the Bible and prays together.

FAMILY DEVOTIONS

Speaking of reading the Bible and praying together, this too builds a core of love in your family. Different families do devotions in different ways, but in case you've never seen any family devotions, let me describe ours.

After dinner, we'd all fall on the floor and lie there joking and telling stories and laughing for as long as we wanted. That was the first thing. We were not rigid in our schedule and this was possible because we made it clear to the children that the family meal took precedence over studies, soccer practice, music lessons, and all those other things that demand our children's time as they are growing up.

Of course we failed at this quite often. Throughout our children's childhood, we rarely had a sit-down dinner with family devotions more than three or four days a week. You say that's a failure—that it ought to have been seven days a week—and I commend you for your zeal. Godspeed.

Anyhow, those days when we were eating together, we did not clean up the kitchen before family devotions, nor did we usually even clean off the table first. Instead we all flopped on the floor. This one had his head on that one's stomach and the other one laid on his side and the youngest bounced from older brother to older sister, then back again. Often Dad played dragon or bucking bronco with one of the younger children on his back, bouncing the little one off onto the carpet amid gales of laughter. But the important thing was that we did what we wanted and what we wanted was to play.

And to touch—I cannot emphasize this too much. A side note here about touch:

Touch is absent between too, too many fathers and their children. Love requires touch. It's so in the church: the Apostles Peter and Paul command Christians to "greet one another with a holy kiss." This command is given five times (Rom 16:15; 1 Cor 16:20; 2 Cor 13:12; 1 Thes

5:26; 1 Pt 5:14), so for what good reason have we banished the holy kiss from our church life today? Did you ever notice how the Apostle Paul said goodbye to the Ephesian elders at Miletus?

> When he had said these things, he knelt down and prayed with them all. And they began to weep aloud and embraced Paul, and repeatedly kissed him . . . (Acts 20:36–37)

Did you get that? They "repeatedly kissed him."

Loving touch is part of the core curriculum in the church, and even more in the home. Yes, the kiss must be holy. There must not be even a hint of lust in the church or home. But why allow the filth of our culture to suppress the holy kiss between brothers in Christ, between fathers and children in the home? The best antidote against bad touch is good touch, holy and loving and tender touch.

One of the pastors in our church is Dave Curell. Dave is an ox of a man, both in size and physical strength. Recently he hit a hole while he was driving his small Ford tractor and the tractor threw him off. When he told me the story, my sympathies weren't with Dave, but with the ground he landed on. He assured me, though, that the ground survived.

Somehow I learned one of Dave's family secrets, and it has endeared Dave and his family to me more than almost anything else. Dave will lie down on the floor and ask his family to lie on top of him.

Why?

He says he likes to feel their weight.

Now Dave is the man who carries the heaviest load of any of our pastors and elders in pastoral care. Like the Apostle Paul, he never stops admonishing and encouraging the flock, house to house, day and night, with tears. If there's difficult work to be done, Dave's the shepherd who sees it and does it.

You see it, don't you? God has made Dave to carry lots of weight. God made him an ox, and, loving the God who made him as he is, Dave relishes the work God has given him—even to the point of having his beloved wife and children lie down on top of him. So he can feel their weight.

Now I will grant you that this kind of physical love and tenderness is a little strange. Likely you don't know any other Christian father who loves his wife and children in this way, but if you knew Dave, it wouldn't seem strange at all. The godly ox takes joy in his oxhood, just as the godly songbird takes joy in her singing and the godly guitarist takes joy in his vibrato.

Anyhow, enough about touch.

After lying on the floor, talking, joking, and roughhousing for a while, our family would read the Bible and pray. That's it. That's all I'm going to tell you about our family devotions. Figure the rest out on your own.

I'm not going to give you a curriculum to follow. Just do it. Keep it short and simple and humble. God will bless you. And if at first it feels awkward, persevere. He'll show you the way.

CHAPTER 13

CHURCH FATHERS

You are witnesses, and so is God, how devoutly and uprightly and blamelessly we behaved toward you believers; just as you know how we were exhorting and encouraging and imploring each one of you as a father would his own children, so that you would walk in a manner worthy of the God who calls you into His own kingdom and glory.

1 Thessalonians 2:10–12

THIS CHAPTER is addressed to church fathers—that is, pastors, elders, and deacons. Sunday school teachers, too. And more broadly, any wise older (or even younger) man in the church with other men, women, and children under his care. If that's not you (and it probably is, in one way or another), I encourage you to read this chapter all the same. The many types of fatherhood are so integrally linked that I think you'll learn something anyway.

Pastors and elders are fathers of the church.

Since the earliest days of the wilderness wanderings of the sons of Israel when Moses appointed elders for every group of ten (Ex 18:13–27), to the age when the apostles appointed elders for every church (Ti 1:5), those who belong to God are settled in the household of faith where their heavenly Father has provided them spiritual fathers. The Apostle

Paul ministered in this way to the members of the Corinthian church, referring to them as his "children" and himself their "father":

> I do not write these things to shame you, but to admonish you as my beloved children. For if you were to have countless tutors in Christ, yet you would not have many fathers, for in Christ Jesus I became your father through the gospel. (1 Cor 4:14–15)

Likely the son of an unbelieving father,[1] Timothy also received such ministry. Adopted by God, he was placed in the household of faith under the care of the Apostle Paul who corrected, rebuked, encouraged, and loved him as a father his own son. Thus the Apostle Paul showed fatherly tenderness, calling Timothy his "beloved and faithful child in the Lord" (1 Cor 4:17).

To this day, God places every believer in this same household of faith where he or she is granted the privilege of receiving fatherly care from pastors and elders.

Samuel Johnson spoke of the weight of shepherding souls this way:

> The life of a parson, of a conscientious clergyman, is not easy. I have always considered a clergyman as the father of a larger family than he is able to maintain. I would rather have Chancery suits upon my hands than the cure of souls. No, Sir, I do not envy a clergyman's life as an easy life, nor do I envy the clergyman who makes it an easy life.[2]

The weight of a pastor's duty is the weight of fatherhood.

Now I only have one chapter to open up the overwhelming nature of church fathers' responsibilities, so let's focus on two aspects of fatherhood that are critically important: discipline and tender affection.

DISCIPLINE

Twenty-five years ago, I was the pastor of a yoked parish serving two congregations eight miles apart, one in a small town and the other out in the country sandwiched between dairy farms just off the right-of-way of the state highway. For years, the country church had been keeping on its membership roll families that never attended church except maybe an occasional Easter morning or Christmas Eve.

Recognizing our biblical responsibility to go out house to house, warning these souls, the elders undertook their duty with fear and trembling and sickness unto death. Splitting up the names and families, we started to visit each home. With diligence we worked through the list, speaking to each person about his soul and inquiring whether something or someone within our congregational life had offended him, causing him to stop attending. Before leaving, we read a fitting portion of Scripture and prayed for the family. And we made it clear that we wanted and expected to see them in church in the weeks to come.

Certainly none of us involved in this work would claim that we did our visits perfectly. Our word choice wasn't always the best, and certainly we failed to demonstrate the depth of love Christ showed to His own disciples. As we did our work, we were jars of clay, but jars of clay seeking to be faithful in all our responsibilities—not just the easy ones. And so we set out to discipline our flock, including those who felt that having their names on the roll of a Christian church and returning to that church each time they had babies to be baptized, sons and daughters to be married, and grandmothers and grandfathers to be buried, was the normal Christian life and guaranteed their soul's eternal protection.

The results were predictable. Immediately, some souls returned to the sheepfold where they were greeted with joy. Others needed another push six months to a year later before they returned. Some returned at first but then became sporadic in their attendance and were visited again and again; the spirit was willing but the body was weak. Some cursed us and began gossiping in the community, lying about what we had said and how we had said it.

When some who had heard this gossip called the elders, we explained that none of us wanted to see these persons leave the church; in fact, just the opposite—we were trying to restore them to our fellowship. We commended our consciences to every man as we had occasion, reminding the congregation of their membership vows and their duty to keep those vows. We went back to the offended parties, delicately trying again to explain our concern over their souls and our desire that they return to the fold. But with a number of those offended, it was to no avail.

After several years of pursuing this work, the time came to remove the names of ten or fifteen people from the list of active members. The authority for this lay within the board of elders, but one family decided to come to the annual meeting that year and publicly oppose the elders' action.

The day for the annual meeting arrived, and following our potluck meal I called the meeting to order and we proceeded through our agenda. Eventually it was time for our clerk of session to report on our membership and the battle was joined. Using every tactic at hand, the offended family stood and fought, accusing the elders of being un-Christian, unloving, hypocritical, judgmental, and even un-American. With meekness and humility, though, the clerk of session (speaking for all the elders) held his ground.

Two things came of this, one predictable and the other astounding.

Predictably, a number of people left the church. We knew this was a probable consequence of our work but we still found it painful. As our overall attendance declined, though, one sub-group began to grow until its presence was the most noticeable thing about our fellowship. Each Sunday morning, halfway back on the left side of the church, young men between the ages of fifteen and twenty-five began to fill up a row and a half of pews.

It was stunning, really, since a number of these men had not been raised in the church. We noticed their presence and began to talk about it, trying to figure out why they were there. Yes, we had a vital youth ministry that extended beyond our own congregation to the youth of a number of community churches, but that had been going on for several years and couldn't have been the whole story. And yes, we had a family in our fellowship that lived in a nearby town and ministered to the young people of that town, having them into their home and around their table. But again, that had been going on for some time and couldn't have been more than a small part of the explanation.

Then it hit us: these young men started coming after the infamous congregational meeting. They had heard about the fathers of the church disciplining their congregation and the father-hunger in them led them to a congregation where there were real men showing faithfulness in discipline, even at significant personal cost.

Watch *Hoosiers*, my state's favorite movie, and you will see this same theme: as the coach restores discipline to his basketball team, the townspeople gnash their teeth but the players fall in love with their coach and begin to win. So when a vote is taken to fire the coach, the players defend him and he stays on. As we watched the movie, my daughter observed that the coach as father is at the center of the sports movie genre.

The purpose of the story of the membership roll is not to argue that elders across the country ought to go and do likewise. There are many different forms of polity within our congregations, and disciplinary action appropriate in one church may well be inappropriate in another. Rather, I tell this story as a testimony to the power of God to use sinful men who are willing to be obedient to their duty to discipline God's flock.

Were I to speak to pastors and elders about nothing else, I would emphasize the crucial witness of loving and firm discipline within the body of Christ, carried out by men who themselves have known and learned to love the discipline of their heavenly Father.

In Acts 20 we read the Apostle Paul's farewell charge to the Ephesian elders. There Paul characterizes his own work among the flock at Ephesus as follows: he served the Lord "with tears and with trials" (v. 19); he "did not shrink from declaring to [them] anything that was profitable, . . . and night and day for a period of three years [he] did not cease to admonish each one with tears" (vv. 20, 31). He also makes this stunning claim: "I testify to you this day that I am innocent of the blood of all men" (v. 26).

Honestly, what pastor or elder among us could think of making such a claim—that we have no bloodguilt because we have been faithful shepherds warning our sheep house to house and day and night, with tears?

Why this neglect? Is it because we are trying to demonstrate the doctrines of grace in our pastoral relationships? Is it because we are seeking to lead our flock to the One who is meek and gentle of heart, in whom we shall find rest for our souls? Why is there such an oppressive silence in our seminaries, bookstores, pulpits, and church board rooms on this subject of discipline? Can it be that Christians have evolved to the point that we no longer need this proof of our heavenly Father's love?

No. Rather, I fear our talk of grace and parallel neglect of discipline are too often the products of our aversion to conflict, our fear of a drop in attendance and giving, and our dread of dismissal. Richard Baxter understood pastors when, back in 1656, he first published his classic work on pastoral ministry, *The Reformed Pastor*. Concerning pastors' neglect of discipline, he wrote:

> It is a sad case, that good men should settle themselves so long in the constant neglect of so great a duty. The common cry is, "Our people are not ready for it; they will not bear it." But is not the fact rather, that you will not bear the trouble and hatred which it will occasion?[3]

Pity the home and church where fathers, finding in their hearts no love for their sons, cast them off without the benefit of discipline. And pity the sons who grow up yearning for this proof of their sonship.

If we ourselves have had the privilege of knowing the disciplinary love of God, let us reclaim that same ministry of discipline for our flocks, giving ourselves wholeheartedly to this duty. And let us trust that God's servants doing God's work using God's tools will never lack God's blessing and protection.

TENDER AFFECTION

As a pastor, I've cared for many men who lacked their fathers' discipline. Similarly, their fathers often failed to nurture them with tender affection.

This is not to say their fathers never tucked them in at night or gave them a playful jab on the shoulder. Rather, as the son grew, he never had the privilege of burrowing into the fertile black soil of clear outward demonstrations of affection—the kind of thing that every son is mortified to see other fathers doing but wishes his own father would give him.

Back in the mid-eighties, my father was speaking at a chapel service at Wheaton College. In passing, he mentioned his conviction that college students wanted their fathers to hug and kiss them. To his surprise, the comment provoked a standing ovation.

Happily, my father practiced what he preached. He was a frequent traveler and how distinctly I remember meeting him in the middle of the concourse at O'Hare, throwing our arms around each other and kissing in front of hundreds of suits, starched shirts, and ties. Standing there in my father's loving embrace, I confess that I thought, *Eat your hearts out, men; I love my dad and my dad loves me.*

American men are so stingy with their affection, robbing our sons of the warmth of human fatherly affection which is so necessary to their emotional well-being. This is not the way of Scripture.

Look into the Bible and see how its pages are filled with emotion—tears, affection, and love. See Joseph as he falls on Jacob's shoulders crying tears of joy upon his reunion with his father (Gn 46:29–30). See Jesus as He weeps at the grave of His dear friend, Lazarus (Jn 11:35). See Him again as He receives (and defends) the tearful and unseemly ministrations of the sinful woman at the home of Simon the Pharisee (Lk 7:36–50). See Him as He pleads with His three much-loved disciples to stay awake, to watch and pray with Him as His hour draws near (Mt 26:36–46). See Paul as he bids the Ephesian elders a final farewell there on the beach at Miletus. We read that, after giving them their charge, Paul "knelt down and prayed with them all. And they began to weep aloud and embraced Paul, and repeatedly kissed him, grieving especially over the word which he had spoken, that they would not see his face again. And they were accompanying him to the ship" (Acts 20:36–38).

What signs of tender affection do our congregations see between their pastor and elders? Would there ever be an occasion when they might see a scene in our own church foyers or parking lots similar to the scene of Paul's departure from the Ephesian elders?

Somehow the church has been misled into abandoning feelings and emotions. Still, fatherhood proves itself through tender affection, and sons of the church who have grown up in a harsh and loveless home that lacks discipline will respond to spiritual fathers who correct, rebuke, and encourage them with tenderness and love.

In celebration of Father's Day 2002, the *New Yorker* carried an autobiographical essay by actor Steve Martin. The piece began:

In his death, my father, Glenn Vernon Martin, did something he could not do in life. He brought our family together.

After he died, at the age of eighty-three, many of his friends told me how much they loved him—how generous he was, how outgoing, how funny, how caring. I was surprised at these descriptions. I remember him as angry. There was little said to me, that I recall, that was not criticism. During my teen-age years, we hardly spoke except in one-way arguments—from him to me. I am sure that the number of words that passed between us could be counted. At some point in my preteens, I decided to officially "hate" him. When he came into a room, I would wait five minutes, then leave. . . .

Generally . . . my father was critical of my show-business accomplishments. Even after I won an Emmy at twenty-three as a writer for "The Smothers Brothers Comedy Hour," he advised me to finish college so that I'd have something to fall back on. Years later, my friends and I took him to the première of my first movie, "The Jerk," and afterward we went to dinner. For a long time, he said nothing. My friends noted his silence and were horrified. Finally, one friend said, "What did you think of Steve in the movie?" And my father said, "Well, he's no Charlie Chaplin."[4]

Picture Steve Martin (or millions of young men like him) walking through the doors of the church and finding in her fellowship the fatherhood of God in all its beauty, lived out by older men ready to give the encouragement and affection Martin's father lacked the strength to provide.

Those willing to give themselves to this work, as well as the work of loving discipline, must not be naive. There are some in our congregations who, due to the destructive influence of their own father, stepfather, professor, pastor, or priest, have been hardened in their hostility toward fatherhood. Fatherhood has never been for the timid. As I mentioned earlier, "There's only one adventurer in the world . . . the father of a family. Even the most desperate adventurers are nothing compared with him." Under the guise of pastoral sensitivity, pastoral leaders will be tempted to make concessions to the spirit of our age. Still, our courage must not fail.

The faithful shepherd will lead the sheep in his flock to confess with all Christians, everywhere, "I believe in God the Father Almighty." And having made this confession, he will work hard to discipline and love his sheep to the end that they will come to grow in their love for the Father from whom all fatherhood gets its name. Father-hunger presents Christians with a wonderful opportunity to testify that fatherhood is, indeed, at the "great world's core." May we confess this, especially as church fathers, with sensitivity and courage, refusing to turn away in shame.

CHAPTER 14

CITY FATHERS

And Job again took up his discourse and said,
"Oh that I were as in months gone by,
As in the days when God watched over me;
When His lamp shone over my head,
And by His light I walked through darkness;
As I was in the prime of my days,
When the friendship of God was over my tent;
When the Almighty was yet with me,
And my children were around me;
When my steps were bathed in butter,
And the rock poured out for me streams of oil!
When I went out to the gate of the city,
When I took my seat in the square,
The young men saw me and hid themselves,
And the old men arose and stood.
The princes stopped talking
And put their hands on their mouths;
The voice of the nobles was hushed,
And their tongue stuck to their palate.
For when the ear heard, it called me blessed,
And when the eye saw, it gave witness of me,
Because I delivered the poor who cried for help,
And the orphan who had no helper.

The blessing of the one ready to perish came upon me,
And I made the widow's heart sing for joy.
I put on righteousness, and it clothed me;
My justice was like a robe and a turban.
I was eyes to the blind
And feet to the lame.
I was a father to the needy,
And I investigated the case which I did not know.
I broke the jaws of the wicked
And snatched the prey from his teeth."

Job 29:1–17

YOU'VE BEEN READING the quotes from Scripture in this book, right? You don't skip God's Word to get to man's, do you?

Did you notice where Job's reputation of godliness was on display? Job says, "When I went out to the gate of the city, when I took my seat in the square, the young men saw me and hid themselves, and the old men arose and stood."

The "city gate" and "square" were the public spaces where decisions were made, business transacted, and controversies resolved. They were the places men did business deals and sat in deliberation and judgment. The life there was public in the sense that it was neither the home nor the church. It was a combination of Speakers' Corner in London's Hyde Park, or Chicago's Bughouse Square, and the courtroom of your county courthouse.

In this chapter, we're focusing on the city gate as the third of three spheres of life and authority—the home, the church, and the city— where the Christian man is called to be a father in the image and likeness of our Father Almighty.

When Dad gave my ordination charge on behalf of John Knox Presbytery, this was one part of his charge:

Be a responsible citizen in your community. Let your influence for ethics and morality be felt, always remembering that the community cannot be held to the standards of Christ's church.[1]

Dad and Mud were not simply private Christians. Their faith went far beyond their driveway and church pew. Wherever they lived, they were responsible citizens, public Christian citizens. It would take a book to record these things but here are a few examples.

Our home housed the needy. The unwed mother, the single woman, the alienated adoptee needing a break from her adoptive parents' home, missionaries, and aged grandparents all found a home with Dad and Mud. Many Lord's Days our table was full with souls gathered into their loving home. Holidays were raise-the-roof-beam times. There was never enough space for all of us. Beyond this, Mud gave decades of her life to leading neighborhood Bible studies during which women came to know and follow Jesus Christ.

For at least ten years, Dad and Mud led a weekly Bible study at a local nursing home. When we were in town, Mary Lee and I would go to the Bible study with them. The nursing home was huge, dark, and full of forlorn souls. Fifteen or so men and women regularly attended the study, and each week Dad and Mud brought cupcakes or cookies Mud had made, along with a drink. Birthdays were special: after a boisterous singing of "Happy Birthday," there was always a cake.

But Dad's public Christian leadership extended beyond our neighborhood and the village of Bartlett, Illinois, where we lived. Some of you may be old enough to remember Dad's writing. Others may never have heard of him. During his life, Dad used his pen as a force for truth and justice. He made no friends when he exposed Christian hypocrisy, warned against feminism, called out Christian physicians for refusing to stand against the slaughter of abortion, or publicly admonished powerful evangelical leaders like Bill Gothard, Bob Jones, and religious celebrities promoted by *Christianity Today*. It grieved Dad to experience the hostility of those who resented his public admonitions, but he kept at the work and when his voice went silent, many within the evangelical church told us how much they missed him.

Back in the fifties and early sixties, long before it was the fad it is today, Dad and Mud took public stands against the racism that was so pervasive among white evangelical Christians. Dad won few friends in the board meeting of the Christian school he and Mud helped found when he stood firm in his demand that the school accept black students for enrollment. My sister Deborah remembers the hostility towards Dad and Mud on the part of her elementary school friends when black children started attending the school. She knew her classmates were simply reflecting their parents' resentment.

Then, in the late sixties when the Civil Rights Movement had begun to change America and black–white hostilities were at a fever pitch, Dad's witness as a Christian father in the public square took a slightly different form. We had a friend who worked in the inner city of Chicago, and through her kindness we gained a young black friend who came to stay with us each summer. With his family, he lived in the Robert Taylor Homes on Chicago's south side. It was a time when there was no love lost between suburban whites and inner-city blacks.

I remember driving with Dad into the city to pick Anthony up. We parked outside those sixteen-story high-rises and walked into the quadrangle of one of Chicago's worst housing projects. Dad and I were the only white faces in sight. We made the trek into the commons at the center of the high-rises, took the awful elevator stinking of urine up to the thirteenth floor, walked down the catwalk attached to the exterior of the building facing all the other buildings, down to its very end, while everyone watched the white man and his young boy. I remember my fear, but it was good to share this work with Dad.

Such things were the nuts and bolts of Dad's witness in the city gate. Once again, I am ashamed to think how much less I have done for the poor and needy, for truth and justice and mercy, than Dad and Mud.

Why am I bragging about Dad and Mud?

Actually, I don't think I'm bragging. I'm sharing. Good examples of city fathering will be few and far between for many of you, and I want to share some of mine.

Well, maybe I'm bragging—just a little.

THE GOOD SAMARITAN

In His parable of the Good Samaritan, Jesus introduced us to a godly city father. I'm sure you know the story. The man who really loved his fellow man, the man who was a good father, even to a stranger in his community, was the man who helped him. And I'm sure you remember the uncaring men who did not stop to help their brother in need. What sort of excuses might we make if we came across a man left for dead by thieves today?

—*Uh, right, Jesus; we should love our neighbor as we love ourselves. But you know, right now I'm working on loving myself. And you know, it's hard work! I grew up in a broken home . . .*

—*You know what, Jesus? My parents never took me to church or Sunday school. I grew up in a single-parent home. Men came and went every couple of months and "God" was a curse word, so I'm trying to change all that in my home. We have family devotions every morning, we're a part of a family-centered church and we homeschool. I run my own business, so between family dinner and homeschooling and co-op and flute and piano lessons and gymnastics and soccer and church and my business, I pretty much fall into bed every night . . .*

—*We're committed to having as many children as the Lord chooses to bless us with, so my wife doesn't have a minute to call her own. We've had seven kids in ten years—it's been forever since she and I got away alone together. I know I'm supposed to love my neighbor. But honestly, where's the time? . . .*

—*Part of the reason we live out here in the country is so we can get away from the world's bad influences. Some of the people around here are meth addicts and I really don't want them in our home. I don't want them around my wife or children. I'm afraid if I stopped at their house to meet them, someone might light a cigarette and the whole place would blow up. You know? . . .*

—*Listen, Jesus. You know what? I don't think my so-called "neighbor" is that lousy bum out walking the traffic island in the middle of the intersection trying to make people feel sorry for him with that sign asking for money. He can work just as good as me. Why doesn't he? You know he's gonna spend the money on booze or drugs. He's not my neighbor! . . .*

—I've thought carefully about this whole thing, Jesus. Poverty is not an economic problem. It's a spiritual problem with a spiritual solution. Real poverty isn't hunger or thirst or limited medical care. It's dying without faith in Jesus Christ. We need to give our attention to the first things. We've gotta be Gospel-centered. We can't spend our time rearranging the deck chairs on the Titanic when souls are dying and going to Hell . . .

—Jesus, think of all the so-called Christians who have turned away from witnessing to the Gospel, instead talking about social justice, healing the planet, sustainability, and global warming. Is that what this is all about? Are You just telling me to engage in more liberal do-goodism? . . .

You see how many ways we justify our cold hearts? We love ourselves quite well, thank you. Meanwhile, we're absolutely convinced we have no money or time or energy to love any outsider. We think most of Christian living is simply keeping our own marriage and home intact.

Jesus wants us to understand that being a neighbor to a man in need is not a duty, but a privilege. Instead of trying to limit our compassion, we're to live by faith trusting God to give us everything we need as we look for opportunities to serve, love, and show compassion in the nasty public world outside our clean homes and churches.

It's our privilege to take responsibility for others, especially others from the wrong side of the tracks, others lacking visas, others who worship a false god, others whose problems are overwhelming to us and will likely bankrupt us if we stop to ask how we may help. This is our privilege.

This is what God did for us.

See how great a love the Father has bestowed on us, that we would be called children of God; and such we are. (1 Jn 3:1)

Our Father is unbelievably liberal with His love, isn't He? If we are commanded to be like Him, why are we so conservative? When He has been so tender and compassionate, sending His only begotten Son to die for sinful man, how can we be so stingy? Why are we so tight-fisted? Look, the world doesn't have enough bandwidth on the web or ink and paper to print all the excuses we self-professed Christian men use to justify ourselves in our lovelessness. Can we not commit ourselves to hear Jesus' story and to learn what He intended to teach us by our hero, the Good Samaritan?

THE GODLY CITY FATHER TODAY

What does this mean for Christian fathers?

The godly father takes responsibility beyond the borders of his own home and church. He cares for his neighbor and takes responsibility for his country, state, city, county, and township. This is what we mean when we talk about the Christian man's duty to be a father in the city gate.

The public Christian father is not stingy, limiting his love and care and protection to those near and dear. He's liberal and openhanded with his love. For him, being "in the city and for the city" is no cheap promotional tool for his church plant. It's not grandstanding.

It's quiet and deep, motivated by his knowledge of the public life of Jesus Christ, the apostles, the martyrs of the early church, and other church fathers down through the ages—right down to the present time. His recent heroes include men like John Piper who was arrested protesting the slaughter of little babies at his local abortuary. Or Clarence Jordan, who fought racism down in Georgia by helping African Americans become farmers and landowners, and who paraphrased a number of New Testament books.[2] Or Chuck Colson, who spent his life in prisons and worked tirelessly for the reform of sentencing laws. I could tell you of many more godly city fathers, but you would never have heard of them and they wouldn't appreciate being talked about in public. Godly city fathers are almost never publicity hounds.

There is no shortage of model Christian fathers in the city gate who stand for justice and mercy. Just look for them and you'll find them in your own county, city, or neighborhood.

NOAH

The Bible tells us, "Noah found favor in the eyes of the Lord." "Noah was a righteous man, blameless in his time," who "walked with God" (Gn 6:8–9). How did he live among his neighbors?

The New Testament book of 2 Peter tells us Noah was "a preacher of righteousness" (2:5). In other words, Noah was audible and visible to the wicked men he lived among. He spoke the Word of God to his neighbors, commanding them, as the Apostle Peter commanded those out in the public square of Jerusalem, to "be saved from this perverse generation!" (Acts 2:40). He built the ark, which served as a visible witness to his faith in God's justice and coming judgment—but also God's mercy and grace to those who put their trust in Him.

The work of the church today seems as ridiculous as Noah's ark did to the watching pagans: "What's *that* all about?" they ask. "What a bunch of weirdos! Look at them—they're building an ark on dry land! As if there's anything to be afraid of. As if there's going to be a flood!"

Yet when a man comes to understand the wrath of God against all ungodliness and the horror of his own sin and guilt; when he comes to see God as He is in all His holiness, and his own heart as it is, depraved and corrupt to the very core; he will begin to search for a safe place.

Just then, there is the church in all her glory. There is the ark of God filled with men who are known in their city as "preachers of righteousness."

Sadly, it seems hard to imagine anyone describing a seeker-sensitive church in this way. And sadly, few of our more conservative churches, either. We have lost our faith in preaching sin, righteousness, and judgment. Within our own cities and evil age, we are not Noah.

PREACHERS OF RIGHTEOUSNESS

Last night I was talking with a man in his fifties. It was a pleasant conversation from beginning to end. We'd never met before and after a few minutes of talking about the NCAA tournament and our respective jobs I asked if he was married. He said no, he'd never married. Then I asked if he had "a woman" and he said he was in relationships with "a couple women." I asked if he went to church and he said no, that his dad had been a United Methodist and his mother a Lutheran, but he wasn't interested in any of it. He didn't care for religion.

Again, the conversation was pleasant—he wasn't trying to bait the pastor. We talked about this and that for a few minutes. He said that before working as a supervisor of heavy construction projects in refineries and steel mills, he'd taught high school, but he'd become very depressed about how many of his students had been abused and molested as children. It was this depression that drove him out of the public schools and into construction work.

So I probed his soul asking, again, whether he'd ever gone to church. He said no, he didn't "need that stuff."

I responded, "What about sin—do you think you sin?"

He said, "No, I'm a moral man. I don't have sin that bothers me. I've lived a good life, done lots of good things for lots of people."

I restrained myself from asking whether both of the women he said he was "in relationships with" would agree if they knew of each other's existence.

Then I asked if he feared God.

He said, "No, I don't have any fear of God at all. If He exists, He can do whatever He wants with me—I'll take my chances. But I'm not interested in religion—not at all."

This is the typical modern man. He has no knowledge of God's holiness, no awareness of the coming judgment, not the slightest clue of the wickedness of his heart and life, and therefore utterly no fear of God. Sure, this particular man was unchurched, at least as an adult, but the same things are true of the majority of those who are in churches in America today.

The fear of God is dead, just as it was at the time of Noah, and what's needed is Christian fathers in the public square who, like godly Noah, will be faithful servants of God joining the work of the Holy Spirit who Jesus tells us is a great blessing because "He, when He comes, will convict the world concerning sin and righteousness and judgment" (Jn 16:8).

This is the first duty of the adopted son of God in his city: he is to be words and actions that convict the world of sin and righteousness and judgment.

Sadly, this work is precisely what most of us are avoiding. We neglect to obey this command of Scripture: "Take no part in the unfruitful works of darkness, but instead expose them" (Eph 5:11, RSV).

We get the first half about not taking part in the unfruitful works of darkness, but the second half—"instead expose them"—is much harder. Yet this is the requirement of our evil day. The world desperately needs Christian fathers who will preach sin and righteousness and judgment to those in bondage to Satan in the hope that some of them will be saved. How will they hear unless someone preaches to them?

But where are the preachers? I'm not simply referring to men ordained to the ministry of the Word, but also to every Christian man living in this dark world. All of us are called to be salt and light, to be witnesses to the holiness of God contained in God's moral law, the Ten Commandments, and to the hope of freedom found in Jesus Christ. We are always to be prepared to testify to this hope within us.[3]

But we don't testify, do we? We're not preachers of righteousness.

There are a whole host of reasons why we avoid exposing the unfruitful works of darkness. Some of us have come up with theological excuses. We say it's the preacher's job to speak for God—not ours. Others are more honest, admitting we're a fraidy-cat. We can't afford to lose our job, or we don't want people to dislike us.

Yet, when we're done with our excuses, we're left with God's command that we expose the unfruitful works of darkness. Exposing is desperately needed today. Sodomy has become mainstream. Homosexuals are getting married and adopting children. Fornication is pervasive both inside and outside the church. Only a minority of those living together bother to marry anymore. Fornicators are not ashamed to murder the children they produce, through abortion. Adulterous remarriages are everywhere. Sexual assaults on children are so pervasive that increasing pressure is coming to bear on age-of-consent laws. Pornography is banal. Greed and envy are the engines driving the world of advertising. Gossip is the main fare of Twitter and Facebook. Women bear arms in defense of their fathers, brothers, and husbands.

So the first thing to say about practical applications of our calling to be fathers in the city gate is that we must give ourselves to the difficult and costly work Noah gave himself to as a preacher of righteousness.

WHERE AND HOW?

What are possible entry points for us becoming preachers of righteousness in our communities?

Start with your conversations. Start personally. Educate men concerning the nature of God's moral law, but also explain the law's interior aspect Jesus illuminated in His Sermon on the Mount:

> You have heard that it was said, "You shall love your neighbor and hate your enemy." But I say to you, love your enemies and pray for those who persecute you, so that you may be sons of your Father who is in heaven; for He causes His sun to rise on the evil and the good, and sends rain on the righteous and the unrighteous. (Mt 5:43–45)

When we testify to God's holiness and wrath against all ungodliness, we must not neglect abhorrent evils like the slaughter of the unborn through abortion out of fear that we'll be seen as engaging in some "culture war" or promoting partisanship of a Republican sort. God Himself hates the shedding of the blood of innocents, so we must say so no matter how quickly people of bad conscience will try to write us off and no matter what accusations they'll make to silence us.

When have Christians ever been able to be faithful preachers of righteousness without being accused of being culture warriors? Of being unpatriotic?

Read through the book of Acts and you will see this accusation:

> For a man named Demetrius, a silversmith, who made silver shrines of Artemis, was bringing no little business to the craftsmen; these he gathered together with the workmen of similar trades, and said, "Men, you know that our prosperity depends upon this business. You see and hear that not only in Ephesus, but in almost all of Asia, this Paul has persuaded and turned away a considerable number of people, saying that gods made with hands are no gods at all. Not only is there danger that this trade of ours fall into disrepute, but also that the temple of the great goddess Artemis be regarded as

worthless and that she whom all of Asia and the world worship will even be dethroned from her magnificence." When they heard this and were filled with rage, they began crying out, saying, "Great is Artemis of the Ephesians!" (19:24–28)

Preaching against a city's lawlessness is dangerous because it will be treated as an attack on the tradesmen and local commerce, as well as the city's gods. The rulers have presided over the wickedness and are likely to see any disruption of the people's trade in wickedness as an attack upon the civil welfare of their city, and therefore an act of atheism or anarchy. This is why, in the first few centuries of the church, Christians were called "atheists" and "anarchists" and were accused of sedition. Salt is salty and light is lighty. Which is to say, there's a reason we want to lose our savor and hide our light under a bushel.

The peace of the Roman Empire was built upon every god of every people group and province being accepted and embraced. It was their pantheon of gods.

Then, along came the Christians preaching to their neighbors and the entire city that there is only one God and one Savior Jesus Christ, that all the gods of the nations are idols and the Lord made the heavens and the earth, that there is only one name under heaven whereby we might be saved, and that name is Jesus; and that this Jesus has been given all authority in heaven and on earth, and He has commanded us to go and make disciples of all men and nations.

The exclusivity of the Gospel of Jesus Christ was absolutely antithetical to the civic religious pluralism and tolerance that Rome's governors saw as necessary to their keeping the peace. This is why Christians were martyred.

They denied their fellow citizens' religions and gods (thus they were charged with atheism) and they were seen as fomenting rebellion against Rome's pluralistic peace (thus they were charged with anarchy).[4]

We are back in that same intolerance and forced pluralism today. We don't expose the fruitless works of darkness because, like the first Christians, we too will be prosecuted for trying to impose our religion and "values" on others.

But buck up. Many faithful brothers and sisters in Christ have suffered persecution in the past. Suffering the same charges today is not the end of the world. Jesus has given wonderful promises to those faithful witnesses who are persecuted for righteousness' sake:

> Blessed are you when men hate you, and ostracize you, and insult you, and scorn your name as evil, for the sake of the Son of Man. Be glad in that day and leap for joy, for behold, your reward is great in heaven. For in the same way their fathers used to treat the prophets. (Lk 6:22–23)

You want a reward in Heaven, don't you? Or do you think it isn't spiritual to seek rewards from God?

Apparently Jesus thought it was quite spiritual to work for rewards. He promised them and told us how to get them, so get to work!

If despite being a follower of Jesus Christ no one in your city and none of your neighbors would think of persecuting you—if you're that kind of "nice guy"—Jesus has something to say to you. Immediately following the previous promise are these three verses of warning:

> But woe to you who are rich, for you are receiving your comfort in full. Woe to you who are well-fed now, for you shall be hungry. Woe to you who laugh now, for you shall mourn and weep. Woe to you when all men speak well of you, for their fathers used to treat the false prophets in the same way. (vv. 24–26)

So you see, for the Christian man, being secure and comfortable and well-fed aren't all they're cracked up to be. Clearly there's something better than laughter. Clearly we shouldn't feel good about ourselves when all men speak well of us.

So says Jesus.

Which way will you face with your fears—man or God?

You can't fear both ways. Choose one or the other.

Of course you'll be misunderstood, sometimes truly but more often intentionally. Godly city fathers have always been misunderstood. If your goal is not to be misunderstood, you'll never be a preacher of righteousness.

We're running out of pages for this chapter, but before we finish I want to mention a couple other things about being a city father.

WORK

Men's lives are defined by our work. This is how God made us.

Work is a gift of God. It's not what we do in order to get our week-ends. It's a joy. It was our calling in the Garden of Eden, in the state of perfection, and we will work in Heaven, glorifying God according to His perfect will. The first thing we must say about work is that it is good.

A man who isn't working is almost always depressed, because work is a blessing from God.

If work is the largest part of our public confession of faith, the Christian man who tries to do his job in a secular way is betraying his faith. We are not Christians in our homes and at church, and non-Christians at work.

This was brought home to me when I was first married.

Mary Lee and I lived in low-income housing on Madison's west side. Across the hall from us lived a woman who, along with her two daughters, had been rescued from her abusive husband by one of the city's women's shelters. We became friends and were able to help her with various needs as time went by.

After a year or so this friend needed surgery. She was operated on a week before Thanksgiving, and after a couple days in the hospital she came home to recuperate. She was not allowed to get up out of bed, so as Thanksgiving approached she and her daughters had run out of food. She asked us to buy some food, so I took her grocery list and filled my cart with the things she needed at the local supermarket.

When I got to the cash register, I placed the contents of my cart on the counter and the cashier rang them up. I took out our friend's food stamps and handed them to the cashier, but she declined to accept them.

This was surprising to me. It hadn't occurred to me that I wasn't allowed to buy her food using her food stamps. When the cashier explained that only the person the food stamps were issued to could use them, it all made sense and I thought, *Well, the manager of this store is a friend from church, so I'll just ask him to approve it.*

I asked the cashier if she would please call the manager, but she replied that he wasn't in the store at that time.

I asked if I could use her phone to call him. Surprised that I knew him that well, she gave me the phone and I called him and explained I was trying to buy food for Joan (not her real name). My friend knew Joan because she'd come to church with us one or two times. He knew she was poor, and also that she had no car.

He said it didn't matter whom the food was for. He could not allow me to buy food for her.

At this point I went into more detail, explaining that Joan was recovering from surgery, was not allowed to get out of bed, and was out of food for herself and her two teenage daughters. Mary Lee and I were leaving to celebrate Thanksgiving down in Illinois with our families and would be gone for four or five days, so the only way Joan was going to have food over the Thanksgiving weekend was if he would permit me to buy the food and take it home to her.

Again, he declined to approve the purchase.

At that point I responded that Christian compassion was never easy and I wasn't over at his store buying food because I had nothing better to do with my time. That if I was taking the time to serve the poor by going on a trip to the supermarket for a bedridden mother, the least he could do was authorize my purchase of her food. (And if you're wondering why I didn't simply pay for it myself, keep in mind this was thirty-five years ago and there were no ATM terminals at cash registers, I carried no checks, we had no credit cards, and we were very poor.)

My friend felt the heat and offloaded his frustration on me saying something like, "Look, Tim, when we're at church, we can think about what honors Jesus. But when I'm at work, I'm an employee of [supermarket chain] and I have rules to follow." Actually, I have to tell you, my recollection is that he said it even more bluntly: "Look, Tim. When I'm at church, I'm a Christian; but when I'm at work, I'm an employee of [supermarket chain]."

To my friend, Christian faith was a hat we put on when we're at home and church, but then a hat we take off when we're at work. That was clear.

There are a few times in life when we seem to have a special inspiration in our response to others. For me, this was one of those times. After hearing my friend out, I made a proposal: "Look, John (not his real name), if you don't want to sell the food to me, how about selling it to Joan? Drive on down here to the store and I can help you load the food into your car. Then you can drive it over to our apartment building and I'll help you carry it up to Joan's apartment and into her bedroom where you will be free to sell it to her, personally. Is that okay?"

John saw he was cornered and said, "Alright, Tim; I'll give my approval to the cashier, but I don't appreciate you putting me in this position. At all."

Joan and her daughters got their food a half hour later and Mary Lee and I were off to Illinois.

The moral of the story isn't Joan and her daughters having food over the weekend, nor is it the tension all of this introduced into the relationship between my friend and me. (Did I mention he was a deacon in our congregation?)

The moral is that everything we do, everywhere we go, every minute of our lives is to be under the Lordship of Jesus Christ and is to be a witness to our faith in Him. Christians are never off duty. We are never free to forget God's truth and justice and mercy, no matter how much pressure we're put under to "take off our Christian hat" and serve our boss, our union, job security, good vibes with our fellow workers, or filthy mammon.

It doesn't matter if you are a union man or management; whether you live in China, these United States, or Morocco. It doesn't matter whether you're rich or poor; whether you work in a public school, a court, a prison, the town hall, the county building, the state capitol, or the White House. It doesn't matter whether you are untenured at a state school or tenured at a Bible-believing seminary. It doesn't matter whether you're self-employed or an immigrant farm laborer.

To be a Christian father in the city gate is to do our work unto the Lord—always and everywhere.

Never forget that the Christian man lives in fulfillment of his Master's commandment, the Great Commission:

> And Jesus came up and spoke to them, saying, "All authority has been given to Me in heaven and on earth. Go therefore and make disciples of all the nations, baptizing them in the name of the Father and the Son and the Holy Spirit, teaching them to observe all that I commanded you; and lo, I am with you always, even to the end of the age." (Mt 28:18–20)

Do you believe Jesus' declaration that all authority in heaven and earth has been given to Him? And, if so, will you have the faith to confess this among men?

It's not a matter of overthrowing governments or getting a conservative Christian elected to the White House. It may happen someday, but it's never our hope.

Rather, our hope is in making disciples of everyone, baptizing everyone in the name of the Father, Son, and Holy Spirit, and teaching everyone to observe everything Jesus has commanded.

Do this with all your heart and soul and mind and strength. Do it in faith that your small and weak efforts will be magnified by His Holy Spirit. Do it away from home and church. Do it in your neighborhood. Do it at work. Do it at the farm co-op while you wait for your feed order. Do it in meetings of the faculty senate. Do it on your blog and Twitter and Facebook. Do it everywhere and always.

All authority has been given to Him in heaven and on earth.

So what are you waiting for?

PRIVATE CHRISTIANS RESENT PUBLIC CHRISTIANS

One final word. Public Christians are always an inconvenience to private Christians, and so we teach young men and new Christians to keep their Christian faith quiet and harmless—which is to say, personal and private. But Christian faith that is personal and private, carefully kept within the confines of home and church, is no faith at all.

No wonder America continues to slaughter babies at the rate of 1.3 million per year, and often just down the street from our church or kitty-corner to our supermarket.

We're private Christians.

No wonder America has come to believe in homosexual marriage. No wonder America has more women getting college, university, and professional degrees than men. No wonder America will soon have a woman president who's a stronger leader than her husband. No wonder America has lost faith in the authority of Scripture, denies the existence of Hell, and never reads the Bible. No wonder America is having fewer and fewer children in homes that are mostly fatherless, now.

Here is Jesus' warning:

> You are the salt of the earth; but if the salt has become tasteless, how can it be made salty again? It is no longer good for anything, except to be thrown out and trampled underfoot by men. (Mt 5:13)

So it's happened, hasn't it?

The world is dying for lack of manly, zealous, biblical fathers like Noah, David, Isaiah, Ezekiel, Hosea, Amos, John the Baptist, the Apostle Peter, the Apostle Paul, Clement of Alexandria, Irenaeus, Cyprian, Augustine, Gregory the Great, Peter Waldo, Francis of Assisi, John Knox, Richard Baxter, Jonathan Edwards, Charles Spurgeon, Dietrich Bonhoeffer, Jim Elliot, Marvin Olasky, Phil Jensen . . .

And Jesus.

PART 4

FATHERHOOD AND FAILURE

Therefore, since we have so great a cloud of witnesses surrounding us, let us also lay aside every encumbrance and the sin which so easily entangles us, and let us run with endurance the race that is set before us, fixing our eyes on Jesus, the author and perfecter of faith, who for the joy set before Him endured the cross, despising the shame, and has sat down at the right hand of the throne of God. For consider Him who has endured such hostility by sinners against Himself, so that you will not grow weary and lose heart.

Hebrews 12:1–3

WHEN I WAS A junior in high school, Dad gave me a gift that to this day forty-five years later sits on top of the bookshelves next to my desk. It's a rough piece of driftwood about an inch thick, three inches wide, and a foot long with eleven crosses made of horseshoe nails soldered together and hammered into the wood. The driftwood has one other item: a very old silver coin glued to the wood down in the lower right corner, just under the crosses. Eleven crosses, one silver coin. On the back Dad used the soldering iron to burn into the wood this inscription:

Christmas, 1970
To Tim, with love from Dad

Dad was calling me to follow Jesus' eleven disciples who were His witnesses and took up their crosses and died. But Dad didn't stop there. Dad affixed the silver coin representing the damnation of the twelfth disciple, Judas, who betrayed Jesus for those measly thirty pieces of silver which were "the price of his wickedness" (Acts 1:18). Dad was warning me not to sell my soul for silver, but to take up my cross and die a faithful witness to our glorious Lord.

God's Son has called each of us to be His witnesses. Are we faithful to His call?

Nowhere is our world's rebellion against God more clear than in its response to fatherhood—God's and ours. If we are unfaithful witnesses, the first place we'll lie about the character and glory of God will be His Fatherhood and ours; His authority and ours. This world is patricidal. It is antagonistic toward fatherhood and any man who witnesses to the Father Almighty by word or deed must take up his cross.

One little example: go to evangelical weddings and listen to the vows. Evangelical pastors across the nation habitually lie by removing the bride's vow to "obey" her husband. Following the pattern of many centuries, when she was married even Princess Diana vowed to obey her husband. But listen closely to the brides' vows in your own church and it's likely you'll never hear a bride vow to obey her husband. Why not?

Because our world doesn't accept the Fatherhood of God. We hide His authority in order to avoid taking up our cross.

We live in the midst of a wicked generation. As you begin to understand something of the fatherhood of God and man, are you willing to be our Lord's witness? Are you willing to be a godly husband? A godly son? A godly father?

In this final section, we're going to talk about bad fathers, and fathers who fail. But as we do, I want to remind you at the outset: tell the truth about the Father Almighty. Be a faithful witness. Be a submissive son. Be a loving husband. Be a tender and careful and authoritative father. It's all about the Gospel. It's all about the glory of God.

CHAPTER 15

BAD FATHERS

For if you were to have countless tutors in Christ, yet you would not have many fathers, for in Christ Jesus I became your father through the gospel.

1 Corinthians 4:15

LUTHER SUMS UP normal fatherhood as "one fool teaching another."[1] There are many who will testify to the truth of his words. Thus, when we give ourselves to the work of fatherhood, immediately we run into souls in the city, home, and church who have had bad fathers and are determined never to be vulnerable to bad fathers again. In our world, there is much bad fatherhood and the damage bad fathers have done is everywhere.

Bad city fathers—judges, senators, mayors, and presidents—have caused many to turn to the political philosophy of libertarianism, the doctrine that the less authority the government has, the better. There are similar positions held by many with respect to the home and church. Since they've experienced and seen men use their authority to the destruction of those under their authority, they oppose all authority. Women abused by their dads marry weak men. Christians who have been members of a church where the pastor or elders were destructive join churches where the pastor and elders do not exercise authority.

Such men and women need to learn a basic truth that's appropriate to remember everywhere in life: the abuse of a thing does not invalidate its proper use.

Hatchets aren't bad because a hatchet was used for murder. Hatchets aren't made for chopping heads. They're made for chopping wood and those abusing them for murder should not cause us to ban hatchets.

The same is true of fatherhood.

Because many fathers abuse the authority intrinsic to fatherhood is no reason to leave fatherhood behind.

As we said before, the authority of fatherhood is everywhere. When God commands us to honor our fathers, He is commanding us to honor not just our own dad but policemen and teachers and judges and pastors and elders and deacons. Fatherhood—of God and of man—is everywhere, and the Fifth Commandment is God's command to us to honor those He has placed over us in the city, the home, or the church.

If we have been abused by bad fathers, how do we submit to fathers later in life without being overwhelmed by fear and making ourselves vulnerable to the continuation of the same abuse we suffered earlier in life, particularly during our childhood? And how do we have faith to become fathers ourselves, exercising the God-given authority intrinsic to our calling? If we don't face the failures of our own bad fathers, it will never happen.

So let's take some time to examine this question.

First, let's acknowledge the ways fathers can be bad.

Many, many fathers today are actual monsters. They rape their daughters and beat their sons. And if the truth is told, many, many mothers know their husbands are doing this to their children and make no attempt to stop it. After years shining light into these situations, often later in the lives of the victims, the elders and pastors of our church have no rose-colored glasses on concerning how often fathers are sexual predators or beat their children, nor concerning how often the mothers of the children have knowledge of the abuse yet choose to cop blindness.

So in the churches I've served there have been a number of sons and daughters who have grown up in homes where they were raped by their fathers, stepfathers, and older brothers while their mother feigned ignorance—often for years. This is very sad, but it's true and must be faced.

But not every bad father beats or molests his children. There are other forms of abuse that are much more prevalent. Fathers who refuse to take responsibility for their children also destroy their children. These are the bad fathers who are never exposed and never disciplined. Those sorts of bad fathers are in the church too. They are the hundreds of pastors who never say "no" and never warn and admonish and rebuke their flock for anything—never and nowhere.

Incest is, of course, horrible. Browbeating and physical abuse of children is wicked. So is the abdication of authority. And abdication is the sin flooding through homes and churches of our time.

Whatever the abuse, whatever the abdication, there are many, many souls in our homes and churches today that have been hurt or damaged by those in authority over them in prior years. It's very difficult for these people to choose to obey their teachers, principals, mayors, presidents, fathers, pastors, and elders. As they see it, the abuse of a thing invalidates its proper use. So they make it their goal in life to keep far away from any vulnerability to authority. They are their own law, their own boss, their own prophet, priest, and king.

It's entirely understandable, and it's entirely wrong.

A lot of the work of the churches I've served through the years has been to seek to restore such men and women to respect for and submission to authority—both God's and man's.

Without submission to authority, there is no holiness. And this is important, because ultimately, without submission to authority, it is impossible to exercise our authority as fathers in any godly way. We have to deal with our fear of authority, our problems with bad fathers, if we're to become good fathers ourselves.

Furthermore, those who claim to submit to the authority of their heavenly Father while refusing to submit to their president, mayor, principal, husband, pastor, or elders are liars. How can we claim to be in submission to our Father we can't see while rebelling against those flesh and blood fathers all around us? It's impossible. Like love, authority's fabric extends from heaven to earth and cannot be sundered.[2]

The woman who submits to God will submit to her husband. The man who submits to God will submit to his pastors and elders. Fatherhood and its authority have been given to us by our heavenly Father for our good, and those who grow up in the home and church without its protection and care are wounded by their father's refusal to take responsibility for them, guarding them from the attack of Satan and his demons.

Get it?

The abuse of a thing does not invalidate its proper use.

So if we're to submit to authority, how do we do so in such a way as not to become vulnerable to every abuse of authority that surrounds us? If our father raped or beat us, how do we bring ourselves to submit to our husband and pastors and elders without getting lost in the black hole of bondage once more?

SUBMIT WITHOUT FEAR

First, let us submit to authority without giving in to fear.

> In the same way, you wives, be submissive to your own husbands so that even if any of them are disobedient to the word, they may be won without a word by the behavior of their wives, as they observe your chaste and respectful behavior. Your adornment must not be merely external—braiding the hair, and wearing gold jewelry, or putting on dresses; but let it be the hidden person of the heart, with the imperishable quality of a gentle and quiet spirit, which is precious in the sight of God. For in this way in former times the holy women also, who hoped in God, used to adorn themselves, being submissive to their own husbands; just as Sarah obeyed Abraham, calling him lord, and you have become her children if you do what is right without being frightened by any fear. You husbands in the same way, live with your wives in an understanding way, as with someone weaker, since she is a woman; and show her honor as a fellow heir of the grace of life, so that your prayers will not be hindered. (1 Pt 3:1–7)

The context here is marriage, with two separate commands given to us by God—one to wives and the other to husbands. First, wives are commanded to be submissive to their own husbands, even if their husbands are disobedient to the word of God.

Our heavenly Father is understanding. He has anticipated our fear of submission. Having commanded wives to submit, He then goes on and, with compassion, He exhorts them not to give in to the fear that is so natural for wives living as helpmates of (always) sinful husbands. Calling wives' attention to the godliness of Abraham's wife Sarah, God tells wives that they have become Sarah's children if they do what is right without being frightened by any fear.

In other words, all of us submit to authority trusting our submission to God who sees and knows all. Nothing escapes Him. Nothing can be hidden from Him. We are to take our fear to Him and trust Him to protect us. We must trust Him to care for us. Even when we're married to husbands who are "disobedient to the word" of God, He commands us to submit to them. And this principle holds true in all relationships of authority and submission.

Radical, isn't it? But being a follower of Christ has never been a tame proposition. To take up our crosses and follow Him is to lose our lives for His sake.

Now, because I've already mentioned it earlier in this chapter, clearly I'm not calling wives to submit to their husband's rape of their daughters or physical and mental torment of their sons. There are evils that godly wives must oppose with everything they have and are, and no evils are more important to oppose and expose than incest and abuse. If you exercise your fatherhood in a wicked way, you should not expect your wife to submit to you.

Such evils will be resisted and exposed by the godly wife.

But we all know there are many matters of judgment in marriage and family life where the wife's judgment differs from her husband's, yet she is called to submit to her husband in that judgment. As in marriage, so in other areas of authority. In our relationships with superiors, we are not to live guided by our own inner lights, refusing to trust our teacher, boss, mayor, husband, or board of elders. We are to be submissive, not giving in to fear. Our obedience and respect for authority is a gift of faith to God and we are to trust Him with our obedience.

EXERCISE AUTHORITY WITHOUT FEAR

If we are to respond to earthly fathers of all types with submission, how are earthly fathers to exercise authority?

There's such a despising of authority in our day that those delegated authority naturally try to avoid exercising it. We know everyone watching is waiting to pounce on our mistakes, so the path of least resistance is to not risk making mistakes, meaning we do our dead-level best not to exercise authority. If a child is screaming in the kitchen while our wife is fixing dinner, we wait to see if the screaming stops. If a woman is having a temper tantrum or slandering others in the congregational meeting, we wait to see if she'll stop. If our wife is being disrespectful of us in front of the children, we take it without rebuking or silencing her. Our philosophy is that it's better never to lead at all than to lead and lose. Thus we abdicate the authority God Himself has delegated to us.

Some may respond that it's not so much fear of the opposition of others that causes them to be silent and allow rebellion to continue as it is knowledge of their own weakness and sin. They have tried to lead and have failed at it again and again. So now they keep quiet and lay low.

This sort of excuse comes up in elders meetings all the time. We have a problem in the church family that we should deal with. We all know something needs to be done, but no one wants to do anything because we're afraid we'll only make things worse, so we sit in the session meeting discussing what could be done and what possible harm would come from doing this or that. Pretty soon, it's clear there's no action that doesn't carry risk of failure—and failure not simply because those we admonish or correct might respond in anger and rebellion, but failure also because we won't get it right. In response to the sinner's anger, we ourselves will get angry. As we work to help others in their sin, we ourselves will sin.

At such times it's important to remind ourselves that, since the Fall, there's never been any perfect father or perfect authority. Every time a father, pastor, or elder takes steps to lead or discipline, before the work is over his own sin has been added to the pool of sin shared by everyone involved. And I'm not being cynical as I write this.

If here on earth we have no abiding place, it's also true that here on earth we have no perfection.

My dad had a saying that was the source of much merriment in our car when we traveled. Noting how resistant men are to admitting our failures when trying to find our way down the road, he'd announce to everyone in the car: "Squaw lost. Papoose lost. Tepee lost. *Indian* not lost!"

Fathers, give it up.

There is no such thing as a perfect authority; no such thing as a perfect act of rebuke or correction or admonishment or discipline. Life on earth is a broken affair. Those who are called to respect authority rebel against that authority, and this makes it even more difficult for the one in authority to bless them by his authority. Those who are called to bless others by the proper use of their authority will sin in the process of exercising their authority, and this will make it even more difficult for those under their authority to submit to them.

But what are we going to do?

Stop submitting?

Stop bearing responsibility for others?

Stop opposing sin?

Stop being fathers and pastors and elders?

Abdicate our thrones?

Here on earth, we have no abiding place. When we say life is corrupted by the Fall, that means you and me. That means your wife and her husband. That means your mayor and the pastor and elders of your church.

God knew this when He commanded us to submit to authority. He knew those in authority over us would add their own sin to the pool of sin as they work with us to protect us and lead us out of our sin. He is not shocked when we fail.

God knew this when he gave us a wife and children, when he ordained us to church office and gave us a flock of sheep to guard and protect. He knew this when He delegated to us the power of the keys and promised whatever we bind on earth will be bound in heaven and whatever we loose on earth shall be loosed in heaven (Mt 16:19).

John Calvin makes a wonderful point over and over again in his writing. He points out that, if God had wanted, He could easily have had angels preach to us and serve as our pastors and shepherds. Instead, He chose to put us under sinful men so we will learn humility and meekness.

Right here and now, it is our calling and privilege to trust God and live the life of faith, submitting to sinful men, and, despite being sinful men ourselves, exercising authority as we ought. For heaven's sake—for the sake of the souls under your authority—throw the stupid ball! You'll never score if you don't throw the ball.

Sure, it might wobble. It might get intercepted.

On the other hand, if you ask God to take your weak wobbly toss and use it for His glory and the protection of His sheep, He will add grace to your weakness and you may see the most glorious success you've ever hoped for in your life!

God is pleased by faithful women who trust Him with their submission to sinful husbands. God is pleased by men who trust Him with their weakness and sin as they exercise the authority He delegated to them.

When we are weak, He is strong. As a matter of fact, He is glorified by using the weak and humble. It's His specialty.

So give up on perfection. Those in authority over you are sinners. And in your own exercise of authority, you are a sinner also. This is the reason God commands us,

> Brethren, even if anyone is caught in any trespass, you who are spiritual, restore such a one in a spirit of gentleness; each one looking to yourself, so that you too will not be tempted. Bear one another's burdens, and thereby fulfill the law of Christ. For if anyone thinks he is something when he is nothing, he deceives himself. (Gal 6:1–3)

Don't deceive yourself. Regardless of the office of father, pastor, or elder you hold, you ain't nothing. Don't think you are.

But realizing you ain't nothing shouldn't ever, ever stop you from working to restore the son or daughter, church member or employee, or even the wife who is caught in any trespass. Roll up your sleeves and be helpful. That's what authority is all about—taking responsibility for others and being helpful.

If you get dirty in the process, think how dirty our Lord got on the cross for you and me. Then rejoice that you are privileged to join Him in His sufferings.

Also, pray lest you be tempted and fall. Pray, too, for those under your authority—that they will love you despite your sins and failures and that they will submit to you without coming under fear's rebellion.

THE SOLUTION TO BAD AUTHORITY

Finally, we must remember that the solution to bad authority is not rebellion against authority, but good authority. This isn't said often enough.

The man in authority is never above being disciplined by another person in authority over him. Husbands and fathers of households are not above being disciplined by city and church fathers. Wives and children are not only to be protected by husbands and fathers, but also policemen, judges, pastors, and elders.

Let me give a couple illustrations.

Some years ago, I got a call from the pastor of the church I'd recently left asking if Mary Lee and I would be willing to have one of the mothers of the church move down to live with us? I said sure, but then we discussed the matter and I found the reason for her moving across state lines was that her husband had beaten her and she didn't feel safe.

"But why should she leave?" I asked. "If her husband is the one who sinned, why should he be allowed to stay in the house while she and the children have to move?"

The pastor and I were close friends, and as we talked it through, it became clear to both of us that the better solution was for the man to leave the house so his wife and children could stay in their home. We continued talking and began to consider the couple's future. What should be done about his abuse of his authority? Who should hold him accountable?

As the conversation continued, we came to a decision that has become foundational in my pastoral work. Felonies should not be handled by pastors and elders. They're the responsibility of the city fathers. Whether it's child abuse, spouse abuse, or incest, the elders of the church must take it in hand and turn the member over to the police. This is our rule.

Why?

Because the Bible tells us our heavenly Father has established governing authorities to be His own ministers to us for good. We are to submit to them:

> Every person is to be in subjection to the governing authorities. For there is no authority except from God, and those which exist are established by God. (Rom 13:1)

In other words, God has given the sword to the civil magistrate to punish evil. We pay his salary through our taxes and we should submit to him in his protective office. So if we try to handle assault and incest on our own, precisely how are we submitting to the civil magistrate as God commanded?

God has been pleased to limit His church officers to moral suasion and spiritual authority. Both powers are real and confirmed by heaven itself, so no one ought ever to take church authority lightly or think rebellion against the officers of the church doesn't matter. It matters, eternally.

But again, God has been pleased to limit the authority of the church to admonition, censure, and suspension of Table privileges or excommunication. He has not given us the sword.

Yet He has given the sword to the city father. God has delegated capital punishment to the civil magistrate.

So when church officers are faced with a woman who is trying to shoot her daughter's boyfriend or a father who is raping his daughters, they are to take it to the police. This is submission to God's authority. God has ordained governing authorities to bear the sword, to "be an avenger who brings wrath on the one who practices evil" (Rom 13:4).

Back, then, to the man who beat his wife.

The pastor met with the elders and they agreed they would require the man to move out of his home so his wife and children could be safe.

They met with the man's wife and told her they wanted her to report her husband to the police. Her husband had committed a crime and they believed the civil authority had to discipline him.

Elders and their wives went to the police with the wife and mother, to report the crime. They also accompanied her to court when the case came to trial. Up until the trial, the man had been denying he'd ever beaten his wife. But at the trial, he saw across the court the pastor and elders and their wives standing with his own wife, supporting her in this terrible ordeal. And knowing their love for him and his wife and children, the man broke down and confessed his sin to the judge, falling on the mercy of the court.

Can you imagine how healing this was to everyone there—particularly the jaded judge and bailiff and policeman, none of whom had ever seen such a thing before?

Here was the church, standing for righteousness by submitting one of their own to the sword of vengeance God had placed in their hands. For once, a spouse abuser was brought to justice and the woman who was abused followed through, testifying against her husband because her elders and their wives stood with her in her weakness.

The solution to bad authority is good authority. Sure, it's not a perfect world, and church officers, policemen, and judges often fail. But that doesn't nullify the plain statement of Scripture that God has given the sword to the civil magistrate, and we are to submit to him. Not just as individuals in paying our taxes, following the speed limit, and pulling a building permit, but also turning criminals within our churches over to him even—and especially—when he is a member of our church and the father of our daughter's best friend.

There's such rebellion against authority today that when Christian women discover God's call to them to submit to their own husband, it's not unusual for that woman and her husband to think that a husband's authority over his wife and children trumps the authority of church officers and civil magistrates. This is a natural error, but it must be guarded against rigorously.

The wife who is so jealous for her husband's dignity and authority that she believes it would be rebellion against him to speak to the elders or their wives about his drunkenness or profanity or use of pornography has not yet learned the nature of authority. She's not the only one in the home who is under authority. Her husband is also.

Just as God has given the civil magistrate sword-authority to cause those who do evil to fear, so He has given officers of His church spiritual authority for the discipline of all her members—especially fathers and husbands.

This is the hope of wives and children who are oppressed by their husbands and fathers. God has placed their husband under authority, himself, and he is to be disciplined so that he does not destroy his charges.

Bad authority is to be disciplined by higher authorities. Failing that, God Himself is watching and will bring those wicked husbands and fathers to His bar of justice.

CHAPTER 16

HE FAILED GLORIOUSLY

> Peter said to them, "Repent, and each of you be baptized in the name of Jesus Christ for the forgiveness of your sins; and you will receive the gift of the Holy Spirit. For the promise is for you and your children and for all who are far off, as many as the Lord our God will call to Himself."

> Acts 2:38–39

AN OLD WAG once said, if a thing's worth doing, it's worth doing badly, so let's end on a negative note.

Not really, but hear me out.

Fatherhood is worth doing, even when we fail. Christian fathers should approach fatherhood expecting to fail—and often. Sadly, sometimes we will fail very badly.

We live in a fallen world and we ourselves are fallen. Yes, we're redeemed, but we are fallen, and sanctification is a lifelong and painful process. We still have within us the law of sin and death (Rom 7:22–23), and this means our best work of fatherhood will remain blighted by sin.

Yet we're not alone in our failures. Failures are all around us, outside as well as inside the church.

Think of King David. Remember his adultery with Bathsheba and his murder of her husband, Uriah? Yet this is the man who wrote most of the prayers of the book of Psalms, and God said this about him: "I have found David the son of Jesse, a man after my heart, who will do all My will" (Acts 13:22).

King David was a man after God's own heart.

As fathers, the best we can hope for is that, in the midst of our sin, God will add His blessing and grace and mercy to our feeble efforts and our sons and daughters will grow up to be godly. Our hope is not in ourselves, but in the Lord who is the Maker of heaven and earth. God is our refuge, an ever-present help in time of trouble. When we are weak, He is strong and He is glorified by working through our weakness.

More specifically, concerning our sons and daughters He has promised He will be a God to us and to our children. Listen to His promise through Silas and the Apostle Paul to the Philippian jailer:

> "Believe in the Lord Jesus, and you will be saved, you and your household." And they spoke the word of the Lord to him together with all who were in his house. And he took them that very hour of the night and washed their wounds, and immediately he was baptized, he and all his household. And he brought them into his house and set food before them, and rejoiced greatly, having believed in God with his whole household. (Acts 16:31–34)

The jailer was told if he believed in the Lord Jesus he would be saved. He was also told his household would be saved.

Sure enough, he believed—and so did his household. He was baptized—and so was his household. He rejoiced greatly—and so did his household.

We must claim this same promise for ourselves and our household, our wife and sons and daughters living with us under our roof and authority. Spiritual life is the beginning and end of Christian fatherhood. Remember what God said concerning Abraham?

> I have chosen him, so that he may command his children and his household after him to keep the way of the Lord by doing righteousness and justice, so that the Lord may bring upon Abraham what He has spoken about him. (Gn 18:19)

God chose Abraham so that he would command his children and his household to keep the way of the Lord by doing righteousness and justice. This was the path by which God blessed Abraham and his descendants.

If you're a Christian, God has chosen you so that you will command your children and your household to keep the way of the Lord. For you, too, this is the path by which God will bless you and your descendants. This is the means by which God will give them the covenant blessings of life in this world, and then eternally.

Claim the promises of God over your own household. Give yourself to the obedience of faith (Rom 1:5) and get to work. Don't allow your sins to silence your commands to your children and your household. God has made you the father of your household and it is your responsibility to lead and discipline and teach and love them as your heavenly Father has led and disciplined and taught and loved you.

Of course you will do your work imperfectly. Of course you will see your failures. Of course you will grieve as you recognize ways you have passed your particular sins down to your sons and daughters. Of course there will be times when your beloved wife will discourage you in your godly fatherhood.

What else is new?

We have our orders and we must carry them out because doing so is life to our children and to our children's children.

So buck up. Don't be a perfectionist. God has been pleased to reserve perfection for Heaven.

Over the years I've been a pastor, I've noticed one of the vulnerabilities of those who have grown up in a broken home is that, when they get married and have their first fight with their wife, they despair. They're convinced cross words indicate their marriage is bad and they're headed for divorce. When they tell me their fears, I assure them that my wife and I both grew up in good Christian homes and our parents exchanged cross words and had fights. Also that we have cross words and fight, ourselves.

But cross words aren't an indication of a bad marriage. They're an indication that the marriage is between two sinners. Also that there are times when we have to work things through in such a way that we get messy. Truth be told, Mary Lee and I are usually more concerned about couples who brag about never fighting than we are about couples who find marriage difficult and argue and snip and snap, getting angry at each other.

God calls sinful men to be city fathers and He is the one who gives them their authority. God calls sinful men to preach to His people. He could have sent them an angel, but it was His good pleasure to send them a flesh-and-blood man with feet of clay.

God calls sinful men to be husbands, and thus it is His will that your wife be loved and led by a sinner.

God calls sinful men to be fathers, and thus it is His will that your sons and daughters be disciplined and taught and loved by a sinner.

All of this is clear.

The life of faith is a life of obedience in the face of our own failures and sin. There's no other way. Don't let the guys with smiley wives and clean pickup trucks and perfect hair fool you. They put their pants on one sinner's leg at a time, just like you. Plus, if you go in their bathroom, you'll find they use liquid plastic to keep their hair perfect. But who wants to walk around with plastic in his hair?

Get rid of any expectation of perfection here on earth. Thorns and thistles grow in homes as well as corn fields. This is life after the Fall, so roll up your pants and shirtsleeves and live by faith.

God could have sent angels to preach to the lost. He could have sent angels to shepherd His flock. He could have sent angels to father our families, but He didn't. Instead, He sent sinful men, so stop being timid and trying to hide at work, out in your garage, or on your computer.

A GLORIOUS FAILURE

My own dad was tender with his children, but he found it easier to preach and speak outside the home than to discipline us. This is not to say we weren't disciplined. Mud had to fill many gaps left by Dad's constant travels fulfilling speaking engagements. But Dad's difficulty disciplining us wasn't simply a function of being out on the road. His temperament also contributed to this weakness.

Dad grew up in the city—first Philadelphia, then New York City.

He was urbane and fastidious, and he was a gentleman. John Henry Newman said, "It is almost a definition of a gentleman to say he is one who never inflicts pain." Newman must have known Dad.

Yet his aversion to inflicting pain wasn't the whole reason Dad avoided disciplining his children.

As I've written earlier, during my childhood, at different times three of my siblings died: Danny, the third born, of leukemia when he was five; Johnny, the fifth born, of cystic fibrosis when he was two weeks; then the fatal wound Dad almost never recovered from—the firstborn, his eldest son Joe.

And, as I wrote before, after Joe died the heart of our home went missing.

God took Joe after a Christmas-night sledding accident. When he died, Joseph Tate Bayly V was a full-ride National Merit Scholar in his sophomore year at Swarthmore College. He was godly and intended to give his life to the Lord's service, yet it pleased the Lord to call him home.

Dad and Mud had a terrible time recovering from that blow.

Of course, I don't mean to imply Dad and Mud stopped loving each other or their children. And yet, family life became hard work, particularly at Christmas. And the severity of this blow was one part of my father's inability to invest himself in the rest of his children for a number of years following Joe's death. By God's grace, my two youngest brothers were barely out of the toddler stage at the time, so when they hit the years of greater emotional need, Dad and Mud had regained equilibrium and things were better.

Skip ahead some years. I had graduated from high school, and after a year at Columbia Bible College I was living at home while holding down a job packing books for a local publishing house. My presence in the home was very disruptive because I was a rebel against God.

As usual, Mud caught the brunt of it. Dad was on the road leaving Mud to cope with my sin.

Then came the day of my father's greatest love for his son.

It was a Saturday morning and I was on my way upstairs to my bedroom. Dad stood on the brick floor of the entryway looking up at me and asked me to stop a moment. He had something he needed to say.

"Tim, you are not honoring God and you may not live in my house any longer."

He didn't raise his voice. There was no drama. It was simply his discipline and my silent acceptance of that discipline. Packing my bags to leave, I was floored by the weight of Dad's action. I wasn't floored by what I had to bear, but by what my father himself bore.

By then, I was his eldest son, and I often took risks that could easily have resulted in my death. Hitchhiking. Foolish mountain hikes. Drugs. Also the fact of my rebellion in the presence of a holy God. Raised in the covenant, I was a covenant breaker and God could have required my life at any time. It was only by God's mercy I remained a living, breathing soul.

Most of this Dad knew, so think of the fear he felt as he prepared to remove his now-eldest son from his house.

Yet Dad chose the fear of God over the fear of the loss of another son's life (much less the loss of that son's friendship).

I can't describe how pivotal this day was in the work of God in my life ever since.

My father disciplined me.

My father loved me.[1]

To this day, Dad's discipline and love stick in my mind as I carry my responsibilities as a husband, father, and pastor. Times without number, God has used the memory of that day to strengthen me when I'm sitting in a session meeting, feeling faint of heart, and with the other elders wanting to avoid using the tool of discipline the Lord has appointed for the protection of His name and His bride. This loving discipline I received as a son often gave me courage when I found myself recoiling from the hard work needed with one of my own daughters or sons.

My dad failed, but he failed gloriously. Dad refused to allow his past sins and failures to keep him from being the father I needed. Dad had faith and trusted God's promises, so he worked and failed and repented and worked and failed and repented and prayed and prayed and prayed.

God honored His promises and rewarded my father's faith.

As we come to the end, please listen to this command from our Lord:

So I say to you, ask, and it will be given to you; seek, and you will find; knock, and it will be opened to you. For everyone who asks, receives; and he who seeks, finds; and to him who knocks, it will be opened. Now suppose one of you fathers is asked by his son for a fish; he will not give him a snake instead of a fish, will he? Or if he is asked for an egg, he will not give him a scorpion, will he? If you then, being evil, know how to give good gifts to your children, how much more will your heavenly Father give the Holy Spirit to those who ask Him? (Lk 11:9–13)

God knows we are evil. Yet He commands us to come to Him for everything we need, even promising our heavenly Father will give us the Holy Spirit if we ask Him to do so. What a good Father we have!

So what do you need, right now? Do you need the Holy Spirit? Do you need wisdom? Do you need help putting to death your lust? Do you need love for your wife? Love for your daughter? Love for your son? Do you need a better knowledge of Scripture so you can do a better job teaching your children the ways of God? Do you need self-control so you can spank your children without anger? Do you need a job so you can support your wife and family? Do you need confidence to stand up to your in-laws when they try to subvert your discipline of your sons and daughters? Do you need faith to hug your teenage son? Faith to ask your college-age son if he's fornicating? Faith to tell your teenage daughter to go back up to her room and change into something modest?

Whatever you need, ask your heavenly Father for it. Right now. He says if you ask, you will receive; if you seek, you will find; if you knock, it will be opened. He promises that if you ask Him for the Holy Spirit, He will send Him to you.

Hear the words of God's covenant with Abraham, our father in the faith:

> I will establish my covenant between me and you and your descendants after you, throughout their generations for an everlasting covenant, to be God to you and to your descendants after you.
>
> Genesis 17:7

NOTES

INTRODUCTION

1. Gail Buchalter, "He Gets the Last Laugh," *Parade*, March 4, 2001, 5.
2. See also Deuteronomy 31:6; 1 Chronicles 28:20; Hebrews 13:5.
3. Question 5, *Catechism for Young Children: An Introduction to the Shorter Catechism.* (This catechism is an excellent tool for teaching Scripture to our children.)

CHAPTER 1 FATHER-HUNGER

1. Oscar Wilde, *The Picture of Dorian Gray* (1890), ch. 5.

CHAPTER 2 THE FALL

1. E. J. Young, *Genesis 3: A Devotional and Expository Study*, (Edinburgh: Banner of Truth, 1966), 79.
2. This question is addressed in the masculine singular form.

CHAPTER 3 THE FRUIT OF THE FALL TODAY

1. This is quite common and often doesn't come out until the victim is well into middle age. When it does come out, it must be dealt with in a way that reassures the woman that there are elders who will not cower in front of the wolf, but confront and discipline him. If crimes are involved and the statute of limitations allows it, the elders must do what is necessary to see that the crimes are reported to the civil magistrate, and punished.
2. Every father of the church should read the accounts of the work Calvin and the other pastors and elders did each week in their con-

sistory meetings back in sixteenth-century Geneva. It would be eye-opening and leave us with an unsettled feeling about the inanity of much of our work in our own elders meetings. See Robert Kingdon, Thomas Lambert, and Isabella Watt, eds., *Registers of the Consistory of Geneva in the Time of Calvin* (Grand Rapids: Eerdmans, 2002).

PART 2 INTRO FATHERHOOD REDEEMED

1. *Confessions* 1.1.

CHAPTER 4 GOD IS LOVE

1. "[Happiness] is the motive of every action of every man, even of those who hang themselves." Blaise Pascal, *Pascal's Pensées* (E. P. Dutton & Co., Inc., 1958; Project Gutenberg, 2006), 113, http://www.gutenberg.org/ebooks/18269.
2. "Sarah obeyed Abraham, calling him lord, and you have become her children if you do what is right without being frightened by any fear." 1 Peter 3:6.
3. John Calvin, comments on Ephesians 5:28.

CHAPTER 5 GOD DISCIPLINES HIS SONS

1. See 2 Samuel 12:13–14.
2. Cotton Mather, sermon on John 5:14 titled "A perfect recovery. The voice of the glorious God, unto persons, whom his mercy has recovered from sickness. Exhibited in a brief discourse to the inhabitants of a place, that had pass'd thro' a very sickly winter, and a time of much adversity. With some remarks on the shining patterns of piety, left by some very young persons, who died in the common calamity."
3. Jim Elliot, Elisabeth Elliot's first husband, who was martyred by the Auca Indians.
4. Excerpt transcribed from Joe Bayly, "Is Holiness Possible Today?

(With a Warning from Esau)," preached at College Church in Wheaton on March 2, 1986. A free audio recording of the sermon is available at http://baylyblog.com/files/old/files/is-holiness -possible-today-with-a-warning-from-esau.mp3.

PART 3 INTRO FATHERHOOD RESTORED

1. NIV (1984 edition). The ESV follows the NIV in relegating "fatherhood" to a footnote. The 1899 Douay-Rheims uses "paternity" while J. B. Phillips and Knox use "fatherhood." The New Revised Standard Version is a liberal adaptation of the Revised Standard Version as the English Standard Version is a conservative adaptation of the RSV. It's sad, then, that the ESV's footnote reads, "Or *fatherhood*," whereas the NRSV simply reads, "Greek *fatherhood*."

2. Word counts for all Bible versions except the 2011 edition of the New International Version were done using *Online Bible*. The 2011 NIV count was done using Robert Slowley, "Word change statistics," last modified November 9, 2010, http://www.slowley.com /niv2011_comparison/all_words.html. There are several modern Bible translations that have not succumbed to feminists' demand that *father*-words be deleted from Scripture. These include the English Standard Version, the Holman Christian Standard Bible, the New American Standard Bible, and the New King James Version. Each is a good choice for those who wish to read all the words of Scripture inspired by the Holy Spirit. Our church uses the NASB (1995 edition).

3. Introduction to the New Living Translation, 1996 edition.

4. Thomas Watson, *The Ten Commandments* (1692; Edinburgh: Banner of Truth, 1965), 122ff.

CHAPTER 8 FATHERHOOD IN ITS PROPER PLACE

1. Abraham Kuyper, "Calvinism and Politics," *Lectures on Calvinism* (Amsterdam: Hoocker & Wormser, 1898).

2. I'm grateful to my dear brother in Christ, Jürgen von Hagen, for

much helpful criticism in the writing of this book, particularly those parts (as here) having to do with Martin Luther. "Iron sharpeneth iron; so a man sharpeneth the countenance of his friend" (Proverbs 27:17, KJV).

CHAPTER 9 HOUSE FATHERS: FRUITFULNESS

1. "For as the woman originates from the man, so also the man has his birth through the woman; and all things originate from God." 1 Corinthians 11:12.
2. "Then Judah said to Onan, 'Go in to your brother's wife, and perform your duty as a brother-in-law to her, and raise up offspring for your brother.' Onan knew that the offspring would not be his; so when he went in to his brother's wife, he wasted his seed on the ground in order not to give offspring to his brother. But what he did was displeasing in the sight of the Lord; so He took his life also." Genesis 38:8–10.
3. Quoted in Steven E. Ozment, *When Fathers Ruled: Family Life in Reformation Europe* (Cambridge: Harvard Press, 1983), 100, n. 2.
4. Charles Péguy, as quoted by James Bemis, *The Wanderer*, June 6, 2002.
5. A good portion of this chapter was first written by my brother David, and I thank him for his help on the doctrine of fruitfulness, as well as for the wise counsel he has given me throughout my years of work in the ministry.
6. "Aren't believers" is not written to say that all those who oppose fruitfulness and discipline are unbelievers. Of course unbelievers oppose these godly things, but sadly, so also do many, many who claim the name of Christ.

CHAPTER 10 HOUSE FATHERS: DISCIPLINE

1. It's worth adding that many Christians today claim all the exhortations to use the rod of discipline are simply metaphorical, and that God is not commanding corporal punishment in these places—only some kind of punishment roughly analogous to the "rod"

used in "ancient times." Read this text again, though, and it's clear this is no metaphorical mention of a "rod." Note the command, "You shall strike him with the rod." A father or mother striking their child can be violence and it can be loving discipline. We must not confuse the two.

2. We won't engage here the question when to start and when to stop spanking. That's a matter of personal judgment, although I know one surly teenager whose life changed the morning he was spanked out in the milking parlor by his father for speaking disrespectfully to his mother. He was sixteen at the time and from that moment he began to grow in godliness.

3. "It was for freedom that Christ set us free; therefore keep standing firm and do not be subject again to a yoke of slavery." Galatians 5:1.

4. "You men who are stiff-necked and uncircumcised in heart and ears are always resisting the Holy Spirit; you are doing just as your fathers did." Acts 7:51.

CHAPTER 11 HOUSE FATHERS: INSTRUCTION

1. The following charts represent statistics from a 2000 study in Switzerland on the likelihood of adult children attending church based on their parents' church-attendance habits:

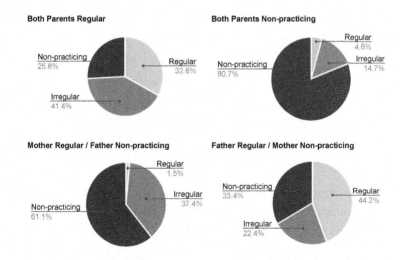

Both Parents Regular
Non-practicing 25.8%
Regular 32.8%
Irregular 41.4%

Both Parents Non-practicing
Regular 4.6%
Non-practicing 80.7%
Irregular 14.7%

Mother Regular / Father Non-practicing
Regular 1.5%
Irregular 37.4%
Non-practicing 61.1%

Father Regular / Mother Non-practicing
Non-practicing 33.4%
Regular 44.2%
Irregular 22.4%

See Werner Haug and Philippe Wanner, "The demographic characteristics of linguistic and religious groups in Switzerland," *The Demographic Characteristics of National Minorities in Certain European
States*, vol. 2 (Strasbourg: Council of Europe, 2000), 154. See also
Robbie Low, "The Truth About Men & Church," *Touchstone*, June
2003, http://www.touchstonemag.com/archives/article.php?id=16
-05-024-v.

2. "The Truth about Education," *What's Wrong with the World* (1910).

CHAPTER 13 CHURCH FATHERS

1. "For I am mindful of the sincere faith within you, which first dwelt
   in your grandmother Lois and your mother Eunice, and I am sure
   that it is in you as well." 1 Timothy 1:5.
2. James Boswell, *The Life of Samuel Johnson, LL.D.*, vol. 3 (Edinburgh: W. P. Nimmo, Hay & Mitchell, 1890), 381. See also Wayne
   Martindale, "Samuel Johnson on the Runaway Imagination,"
   Touchstone, Fall 1991.
3. Richard Baxter, *The Reformed Pastor* (1656; Edinburgh: Banner of
   Truth, 1974), 47.
4. Steve Martin, "The Death of My Father," *New Yorker*, June 17 &
   24, 2002, 84.

CHAPTER 14 CITY FATHERS

1. See "An Ordination Charge to a Son," *BaylyBlog*, July 10, 2006,
   http://baylyblog.com/blog/2006/07/ordination-charge-son.
2. For an excellent biography of Clarence Jordan, uncle of Hamilton
   Jordan who served as President Jimmy Carter's chief of staff, see
   Dallas Lee, *The Cotton Patch Evidence: The Story of Clarence Jordan and the Koinonia Farm Experiment* (New York: HarperCollins,
   1971).
3. "But sanctify Christ as Lord in your hearts, always being ready to
   make a defense to everyone who asks you to give an account for
   the hope that is in you, yet with gentleness and reverence." 1 Peter
   3:15.

4. See Herbert B. Workman, *Persecution in the Early Church* (1906; Bloomington, Ind.: Warhorn Publishing, 2014), especially chapter 2, "Caesar or Christ."

CHAPTER 15 BAD FATHERS

1. "As a rule, the parents, too, are themselves stupid and ignorant; one fool trains [teaches] another, and as they have lived, so live their children after them." *The Large Catechism by Dr. Martin Luther*, trans. F. Bente and W. H. T. Dau (Penn State, 2000), http://www .blaine-grace-lutheran.org/sites/default/files/mllc.pdf.

2. "If someone says, 'I love God,' and hates his brother, he is a liar; for the one who does not love his brother whom he has seen, cannot love God whom he has not seen. And this commandment we have from Him, that the one who loves God should love his brother also." 1 John 4:20–21.

CHAPTER 16 HE FAILED GLORIOUSLY

1. "As a father, when he turns out of his house a contumacious son and deprives him of his presence and the testimonies of paternal favor, still not as yet on that account does he wholly disinherit him or divest himself of all fatherly affection towards him; nay, then using this remedy to bring him to repentance, even by this deed exercises his love towards him although not acknowledging it then, will afterwards acknowledge it, when by true conversion he shall have returned into favor with his father." Francis Turretin, *Institutes of Elenctic Theology*, 3 vols. (Phillipsburg, N.J.: Presbyterian and Reformed Publishing Company, 1994), 3:295.

SCRIPTURE INDEX

GENESIS

1:28 . . . . . .91, 94, 97
3:9 28
3:10 28
3:11 28
3:12 28
3:17 27
4:9 31
5:2 15
6–7 119
6:5–6 32
6:8–9 158
9:7 95
9:20–27 21
17:7 191
17:15–22 95
18–19 119
18:19 186
35:11 95
38:8–10 196
46:29–30 147

EXODUS

18:13–27 141
20:5 64
20:12 . . . . . .79, 115
34:12–14 63

LEVITICUS

26:4 95
26:9 95
26:20 95
26:22 95
26:29 96

NUMBERS

3:4 96
5:28 97

DEUTERONOMY

6:1–2 125
6:3 95
6:4–5 67
6:6–9 . . . . . 123, 126
7:13 95
8:1 95
30:5 95
30:16 95

JOSHUA

1:5 5

1 SAMUEL

13:14 32
25 119

2 SAMUEL

6:36–37	119
11	32
11:1–12:25	56
12:15–23	119
13	32
15–18	32

1 KINGS

1:6	33, 107

2 KINGS

5:13	80
22:13	123

1 CHRONICLES

28:6	43

JOB

29:1–17	151

PSALMS

51	56
51:5	29
103:8–18	24
103:13–14	45, 49
128	100

PROVERBS

3:12	107, 122
13:24	108
23:12–14	108
23:13–14	122
27:17	196

ISAIAH

11:9	47
27:9	58
38:19	123
43:27	25
49:23	80
53:10	91

JEREMIAH

17:9	34
29:6	91
31:29	31

MALACHI

2:15	102
4:6	5

MATTHEW

3:16–4:1	73
4:22	63
5:13	168
5:43–45	161
8:6	80
10:35–38	64
15:6	79
16:19	179
17:5	103
19:4–5	6
26:36–46	147
27:43	75
28:18–20	167

MARK

9:7	75
10:17–18	21
10:28–31	130

LUKE

3:36–38	25

6:22–23 163
6:24–26 163
7:36–50 147
10:39–42 127
11:9–13 191
11:11–13 21
14:26 64
15:21 66
18:19 66

JOHN
1:18 69
2:14–17 74
3:16–17 72
5:17, 19–20 70
9:1–3 57
11:35 147
14:31 71
15:16 99
16:8 159

ACTS
1:18 172
2:38–39 185
2:40 158
2:42 8
2:44–47 104
5:1–10 119
5:11–14 119
5:32–35 104
7:51 197
12:21–23 119
13:22 186
16:31–34 186
19:24–28 161
20:19 145
20:20 145

20:26 145
20:31 145
20:36–37 139
20:36–38 147

ROMANS
1:5 187
3:18 118
3:23 9
5:8 49
7:22–23 185
8:15 29
13:1 . . . . 85, 86, 182
13:4 182
14:23 55
16:15 138

1 CORINTHIANS
4:14–15 142
4:15 173
4:17 142
5:1–2 38
8:6 11
11:12 196
11:27–32 . . . . .56, 120
16:20 138

2 CORINTHIANS
5:17 44
13:12 138

GALATIANS
4:4–6 44
4:6 29
4:26 104
5:1 197
5:14–15 137

6:1–3 180
6:10 8

EPHESIANS
3:14–15 77
4:32 136
5:11 160
6:4 50

PHILIPPIANS
2:6–7, 8 72

COLOSSIANS
3:21 . . . . . . .50, 117

1 THESSALONIANS
2:10–12 141
5:26 138

1 TIMOTHY
1:5 198
2:3, 4 73
3:15 8

2 TIMOTHY
3:16–17 . . . . . .33, 128

TITUS
1:5 141

HEBREWS
9:27 59
10:30–31 121
12:1–3 171
12:6 122
12:6–8 55
12:7 55
12:10 60

1 PETER
3:1–7 176
3:6 194
3:7 50
3:15 198
4:8 133
5:14 139

2 PETER
2:5 158

1 JOHN
1:8–10 133
3:1 156
4:8 48
4:10 48
4:14 75
4:16 48
4:20–21 199

Thank you for purchasing this book!

*To download a **free** digital copy, please visit*
warhornmedia.com/daddy-tried-download

CPSIA information can be obtained
at www.ICGtesting.com
Printed in the USA
LVOW03s1649070917
547917LV00001B/3/P

C000304136

VEGETABLE IDLI

PHOTOGRAPH BY JIGNESH JHAVERI

Chawal

TARLA DALAL

India's #1 Cookery Author

S&C

SANJAY & CO.

MUMBAI

Fifth Printing : 2007

ISBN 10 : 81-86469-85-0
ISBN 13 : 978-8-186469-85-9

Price: Rs. 89/-

Published & Distributed by : **Sanjay & Company**

353/A-1, Shah & Nahar Industrial Estate, Dhanraj Mill Compound, Lower Parel (W), Mumbai - 400 013. INDIA.
Tel. : (91-22) 2496 8068 • Fax : (91-22) 2496 5876 • E-mail : sanjay@tarladalal.com

UK and USA customers can call us on :
UK : 02080029533 • USA : 213-634-1406
For books, Membership on **tarladalal.com**, Subscription for **Cooking & More** and Recipe queries
Timing : 9.30 a.m. to 7.00 p.m. (IST), from Monday to Saturday
Local call charges applicable

Recipe Research & **Production Design** Pinky Chandan Dixit Arati Fedane Pradnya Sundararaj	**Nutritionist** Nisha Katira **Food Styling** Shubhangi Dhaimade	**Photography** Jignesh Jhaveri **Typesetting** Adityas Enterprises	**Designed by** Satyamangal Rege **Printed by :** Minal Sales Agencies, Mumbai

DISCLAIMER
While every precaution has been taken in the preparation of this book,
the publishers and the author assume no responsibility for errors or
omissions. Neither is any liability assumed for damages resulting from
the use of information contained herein. And of course, no book is a
substitute for a qualified medical advice. So it is wiser to modify your
dietary patterns under the supervision of a doctor or a nutritionist.

BULK PURCHASES
Tarla Dalal Cookbooks are ideal gifts. If you are interested in
buying more than 500 assorted copies of Tarla Dalal Cookbooks
at special prices, please contact us at 91-22-2496 8068 or
email : sanjay@tarladalal.com

Introduction

Dear Friends

The simplicity and ease of cooking with rice has made this grain a staple food for more than half the globe.

There are literally thousands and thousands of rice dishes all around the world, ranging from simple everyday fare to delicacies reserved for special occasions. This versatile grain can be enjoyed either hot or cold, as a savoury or a sweet dish. It lends itself easily to the flavours of other foods, and thus forms a perfect base to all kinds of accompaniments.

Rice is savoured in different ways in every corner of the country, each preparation unique and exquisite. It means different things to different people - to a South Indian it may mean cool curd-rice, page 73; for a North Indian, it is the aromatic Vegetable Biryani, page 9.

Cooking rice is an art by itself. Some people always manage to get their rice light and fluffy, with absolutely every grain remaining separate and yet well cooked. How do they do it? Just flip through to page 101 to learn the intricacies of making the perfect rice. Rice used in Indian cuisine can be classified under 3 basic categories Long White Grain Rice - most commonly used for preparations like biryanis and pulaos. Short Grain Rice - used to make khichadis, sweet dishes and fermented rice preparations like the dosas uttpams etc. Round Grain Rice -not very popular in cooking but is used for worship representing Health, Wealth & Fertility.

In this book, I have compiled recipes of my favourite pulaos, biryanis, khichadis , some all-time favourites like the Chinese Fried Rice, page 93 and a couple of desserts.

Happy Cooking !!!

5

Contents

PULAOS AND BIRYANI

Vegetable Biryani 9

Brinjal Rice 12

Gatte ka Pulao 15

Paneer Tikka Pulao 18

Bread Kofta Biryani 22

Nariyalwale Chawal 26

Corn Methi Pulao 28

Soya Mutter Pulao 30

Lilva Rice 32

Paneer Pulao 34

Ghee Rice 36

Lemon Rice 39

Masoor Biryani 41

Cabbage Rice 43

Korma Rice 44

Masala Bhaat 47

Tamarind Rice 49

Aloo Gobi ka Pulao 51

Pearl Pulao 53

KHICHADI

Panchamel Khichadi 57

Badshahi Khichadi.................................. 59

Wholesome Khichadi 62

Handi Khichadi...................................... 64

Ek Top na Dal Bhaat............................. 68

Bisi Bele Huli Anna............................... 71

Coriander Curd Rice.............................. 73

Chitrana Rice 76

Handi Hot Pot 79

Mexican Fried Rice 91

Chinese Fried Rice 93

Risotto Florentina.................................. 94

Spanish Rice... 96

INTERNATIONAL FAVOURITES

Roasted Vegetables with Brown Rice .. 82

Steamed Curry Rice 86

Thai Layered Rice 88

DESSERTS

Sitafal Firni.. 99

Rice Kheer 100

BASIC RECIPES

Steamed Rice... 101

Coconut Milk 102

Pulaos and Biryani

Vegetable Biryani

Picture on cover

* Preparation time : 15 minutes. * Cooking time : 20 minutes.   * Serves 4.
* Baking time : 25 minutes. * Baking temperature : 200°C (400°F).

For the rice
1 cup long grained rice
1 clove (laung)
1 stick cinnamon (dalchini)
1 bay leaf (tejpatta)
1 cardamom (elaichi)
salt to taste

For the vegetable gravy
1½ cups mixed boiled vegetables (carrots, peas, cauliflower, French beans, potatoes),
cut into cubes
¼ cup paneer (cottage cheese), cut into cubes
½ tsp cumin seeds (jeera)
¾ cup onions, finely chopped

2 tsp ginger-garlic paste
3 tsp chilli powder
2 tsp coriander (dhania) powder
¼ tsp turmeric powder (haldi)
½ tsp garam masala
1 cup tomatoes, chopped
1 cup milk
2 tbsp oil
salt to taste

Other ingredients
3 tbsp curds
¼ cup coriander, chopped
a few saffron strands mixed with 2 tbsp of hot water
2 tbsp ghee

For the rice
1. Clean, wash and soak the rice for approx. 15 minutes. Drain and keep aside.
2. In a large pan, boil 3 cups of water with clove, cinnamon, bay leaf, cardamom and salt and then add the rice.
3. Cover and simmer till the rice is nearly cooked. Drain and keep aside.

For the vegetable gravy
1. Heat the oil in a pan and add the cumin seeds.
2. When they crackle, add the onions and ginger-garlic paste and sauté till the onions turn golden brown.
3. Add the chilli powder, coriander powder, turmeric powder and garam masala and sauté for 2 to 3 minutes.
4. Add the chopped tomatoes and cook over a slow flame for 7 to 8 minutes.
5. Add the milk and continue to simmer for 5 to 7 minutes.
6. Add the boiled vegetables and paneer and mix well.

How to proceed
1. Combine the curds, coriander and saffron and mix well.
2. In a deep vessel, arrange the vegetable gravy on the base.
3. Top with the rice and spoon the curd mixture and ghee over the rice.
4. Cover with a tight lid and cook on a tava (griddle) over a slow flame for 25 to 30 minutes or bake in a pre-heated oven at 200°C (400°F) for 20 minutes. Serve hot.

Brinjal Rice

* Preparation time : 15 minutes.　* Cooking time : 20 minutes.　* Serves 4.

1½ cups long grained rice
1½ cups brinjals (baingan), cut into cubes
3 tbsp roasted peanuts
3 tbsp sesame seeds (til)
1 tbsp chana dal (split Bengal gram)
3 whole dry red chillies
5 to 6 curry leaves
½ tsp mustard seeds (rai)
¼ tsp asafoetida (hing)
¼ tsp turmeric powder (haldi)
1 tsp tamarind (imli), soaked in ¼ cup water
2 tbsp spice powder, see below
¼ cup fresh coconut, grated
2 tbsp oil
salt to taste

For the spice powder
1 tbsp coriander (dhania) seeds
1 tbsp cumin seeds (jeera)
1 tbsp chana dal (split Bengal gram)
1 tbsp urad dal (split black lentils)
1 tbsp sesame seeds (til)
6 whole dry red chillies
½ tsp asafoetida (hing)
½ tsp salt

For the spice powder
1. Roast all the ingredients in a pan for 2 to 3 minutes.
2. Grind to a fine powder in a blender. Store in an air-tight container.

How to proceed
1. Clean, wash and soak the rice for approx. 15 minutes. Drain and keep aside.
2. Roast the sesame seeds lightly and coarsely powder the sesame seeds and peanuts in a blender. Keep aside.
3. Heat the oil in a pressure cooker, add the chana dal, dry red chillies, curry leaves and mustard seeds and sauté for a few seconds.
4. When the mustard seeds crackle, add the asafoetida, rice, brinjals, turmeric powder

and half the spice powder and salt and sauté for 2 to 3 minutes.
5. Add 3 cups of hot water and tamarind water and mix well. Pressure cook the rice for 2 whistles.
6. Add the peanut-sesame powder, grated coconut and the remaining spice powder to the rice and mix gently with a fork.
   Serve hot.

Gatte Ka Pulao

∗ Preparation time : 15 minutes.　　∗ Cooking time : 30 minutes.　　∗ Serves 4.

1½ cups steamed rice, page 101
¼ cup onions, sliced
1 cardamom (elaichi)
2 cloves (laung)
½ tsp cumin seeds (jeera)
½ tsp mustard seeds (rai)
¼ tsp asafoetida (hing)
1 tsp chilli powder
½ tsp turmeric powder (haldi)
½ tsp garam masala
1 tbsp oil
salt to taste

To be ground into a paste
4 cloves garlic
2 green chillies

50 mm. (2") piece ginger
¼ cup onions, sliced

For the gattas
1 cup Bengal gram flour (besan)
1 tsp chilli powder
1 teaspon fennel seeds (saunf)
½ tsp ajwain (carom seeds)
1 tbsp curds
2 tbsp chopped coriander
2 tbsp oil
salt to taste
oil for deep frying

For the garnish
2 tbsp chopped coriander

For the gattas
1. Combine all the ingredients and knead to make a stiff dough adding a little water, if required.

2. Divide the dough into 8 equal portions and shape each portion into a 100 mm. (4")
   long and 5 mm. (⅙") diameter cylindrical roll.
3. Boil plenty of water and put the gatta rolls in it. Cook for 10 to 12 minutes.
4. When cooked, drain the water and keep the gattas aside.
5. Cut the gattas into small pieces when cool.
6. Deep fry the gatta pieces in hot oil. Drain on absorbent paper and keep aside.

How to proceed
1. Heat the oil in a kadai and deep fry the sliced onions. Drain on absorbent paper
   and keep aside.
2. Heat the oil in a pan and add the cardamom, cloves, cumin seeds, mustard seeds
   and asafoetida.
3. Add the prepared paste and sauté for 4 to 5 minutes.
4. Add the steamed rice, deep fried onions, deep fried gattas, chilli powder, turmeric
   powder, garam masala and salt and mix well.
   Serve hot, garnished with the coriander.

Paneer Tikka Pulao

Picture on facing page

❋ Preparation time : 15 minutes. ❋ Cooking time : 20 minutes. ❋ Serves 4.

For the paneer tikkas
1½ cups paneer (cottage cheese), cut into 50 mm. (2") cubes
½ cup capsicum, cut into 50 mm. (2") pieces
½ cup onions, cut into thick wedges
½ cup thick curds
½ tsp Bengal gram flour (besan)
1 tsp ginger paste
1 tsp garlic paste
2 tsp chilli powder
½ tsp kasuri methi (dried fenugreek leaves)
½ tsp garam masala
2 tbsp chopped coriander
2 tbsp mustard oil
salt to taste

Paneer Tikka Pulao : Recipe above ➻

For the rice
1½ cups long grained rice
½ tsp cumin seeds (jeera)
2 cloves (laung)
1 bay leaf (tejpatta)
25 mm. (1") stick cinnamon (dalchini)
1 tbsp oil
salt to taste

Other ingredients
2 tbsp oil

For the garnish
a sprig of mint

For the paneer tikkas
1. Combine the curds, gram flour, ginger paste, garlic paste, chilli powder, kasuri methi, garam masala, coriander, salt and 1 tablespoon of mustard oil and mix well to prepare a marinade.
2. Add the paneer, onions and capsicum to it and keep aside for 10 to 15 minutes.
3. Arrange the paneer, onions and capsicum on 4 skewer sticks.

4. Heat 1 tablespoon of oil on a non-stick tava (griddle) and sauté the paneer tikkas till they are lightly browned on all sides (approx. 4 to 5 minutes). Remove from the skewer and keep aside.

For the rice
1. Clean, wash and soak the rice for approx.15 minutes. Drain and keep aside.
2. Heat the oil in a heavy bottom pan, add the cumin seeds, cloves, bay leaf and cinnamon and stir.
3. When the cumin seeds crackle, add the rice and salt and sauté for 2 minutes.
4. Add 3 cups of hot water. Cover and cook over a low flame for 10 to 15 minutes till the rice is cooked. Separate each grain of rice very lightly with a fork and keep aside.

How to proceed
1. Heat the oil in a non-stick pan.
2. Add the paneer tikkas and rice and mix together very lightly. Cook till the rice is hot.
3. Garnish with the sprig of mint and serve immediately.

Bread Kofta Biryani

* Preparation time : 30 minutes.   * Cooking time : 20 minutes.   * Serves 4.
* Baking time : 25 minutes.   * Baking temperature : 200°C (400°F).

For the bread koftas
4 bread slices
2 tbsp finely chopped onions
2 green chillies, finely chopped
1 tsp curds
a pinch soda bi-carb
1 tsp ginger-garlic paste
salt to taste
oil for deep frying

For the rice
1 cup long grained rice
1 bay leaf (tejpatta)
25 mm. (1") stick cinnamon (dalchini)
2 cardamom (elaichi)

2 cloves (laung)
salt to taste

For the gravy
2 cloves (laung)
25 mm. (1") stick cinnamon (dalchini)
¼ cup onions, sliced
2 tsp ginger-garlic paste
1 tsp chilli powder
2 tsp coriander-cumin seed (dhania-jeera) powder
¼ tsp turmeric powder (haldi)
1 cup tomatoes, sliced
½ cup curds
¼ cup green peas, boiled
3 tbsp oil
salt to taste

To be mixed together for the curd mixture
4 tbsp curds
2 tbsp chopped mint
2 tbsp chopped coriander

2 tbsp water

For the bread koftas
1. Combine all the ingredients except the oil with 2 tbsp of water. Mix well.
2. Divide the mixture in 15 to 20 portions. Shape into even sized rounds.
3. Deep fry in hot oil till they are golden brown in colour.
4. Drain on absorbent paper and keep aside.

For the rice
1. Clean, wash and soak the rice for approx. 15 minutes.
2. Boil 2 cups of water, add the bay leaf, cinnamon, cardamom, cloves and salt and then add the rice.
3. Reduce the heat to a simmer, cover the pan and cook till the rice is done. Separate each grain of rice lightly with a fork. Keep aside.

For the gravy
1. Heat the oil in a pan and add the cloves and cinnamon.
2. Add the onions and sauté till they turn translucent.
3. Add the ginger-garlic paste, chilli powder, coriander-cumin seed powder and turmeric powder and sauté for 1 minute.
4. Add the tomatoes and salt and cook for 5 to 7 minutes, till the oil separates.

5. Add the curds, mix well and simmer for a further 5 minutes.
6. Add the boiled green peas and mix well. Keep aside.

How to proceed
1. Spoon out the gravy at the bottom of a baking dish.
2. Top with the bread koftas and cover with the cooked rice.
3. Top with the curds mixture.
4. Cover with a lid and bake in a pre-heated oven at 200°C (400°F) for 15 to 20 minutes.
   Serve hot.

Nariyalwale Chawal

* Preparation time : 10 minutes.   * Cooking time : 20 minutes.   * Serves 4.

1¼ cups long grained rice
1 tbsp urad dal (split black lentils)
2 tbsp yellow moong dal (split yellow gram)
6 whole dry red chillies
5 curry leaves
2 tbsp salted peanuts, crushed lightly
2½ cups (500 ml.) coconut milk, page 102
2 tbsp oil
salt to taste

For the garnish
¼ cup fresh coconut, grated

1. Clean, wash and soak the rice for approx. 20 minutes. Drain and keep aside.
2. Heat the oil in a pressure cooker. Add the urad dal and moong dal and fry for 2 minutes.

3. Add the red chillies, curry leaves and peanuts and fry again for about 1 minute.
4. Add the rice and sauté for another 2 to 3 minutes.
5. Add the coconut milk and salt and pressure cook for 2 whistles.
6. Allow the steam to escape before opening. Separate each grain of rice lightly with a fork.

   Serve hot, garnished with the grated coconut.

Handy tip : You can also garnish this dish with chopped onions and tomatoes.

Corn Methi Pulao

* Preparation time : 6 minutes.   * Cooking time : 8 minutes.   * Serves 2.

1½ cups long grained rice
2 to 4 peppercorns
12 mm. (½") stick cinnamon (dalchini)
2 cloves (laung)
2 cardamoms (elaichi)
¼ cup onions, sliced
1 cup fenugreek (methi) leaves, chopped
½ cup sweet corn kernels
¼ tsp turmeric powder (haldi)
1 tbsp butter
1 tbsp oil
salt to taste

For serving
fresh curds

1. Clear, wash and soak the rice for approx. 15 minutes. Drain and keep aside.
2. Heat the butter and oil in a pressure cooker, add the peppercorns, cinnamon, cloves, cardamom and onions and fry for some time.
3. Add the fenugreek leaves, corn kernels and turmeric powder and stir for a few seconds.
4. Finally, add the rice and 2½ cups of hot water along with the salt and pressure cook for 2 whistles. Allow the steam to escape before opening. Separate each grain of rice lightly with a fork.
   Serve hot with fresh curds.

Soya Mutter Pulao

✳ Preparation time : 10 minutes.　　✳ Cooking time : 20 minutes.　　✳ Serves 4.

1½ cups long grained rice
¼ cup soya nuggets (chunks)
¼ cup green peas
½ tsp cumin seeds (jeera)
25 mm. (1") stick cinnamon (dalchini)
2 cloves (laung)
1 bay leaf (tejpatta)
1 cardamom (elaichi)
½ cup onions, chopped
¼ tsp turmeric powder (haldi)
¼ tsp garam masala
1 tsp coriander (dhania) powder
½ cup tomatoes, chopped
2 tsp oil
salt to taste

To be ground into a chilli-garlic paste
3 cloves garlic
3 whole dry red chillies

1. Clean, wash and soak the rice for approx. 15 minutes. Drain and keep aside.
2. Combine the soya nuggets and salt with 1 cup of water hot and soak for 20 minutes. Drain squeeze out the water and keep aside.
3. Heat the oil in a pressure cooker and add the cumin seeds, cinnamon, cloves, bay leaf and cardamom.
4. When the cumin seeds crackle, add the onions and prepared chilli-garlic paste and sauté till the onions turn golden brown.
5. Add the turmeric powder, garam masala, coriander powder, tomatoes, rice, green peas, soya nuggets and salt and sauté for another 2 minutes.
6. Add 3 cups of hot water and pressure cook for 2 whistles.
7. Allow the steam to escape before opening. Separate each grain of rice lightly with a fork.
   Serve hot.

Lilva Rice

* Preparation time : 10 minutes.   * Cooking time : 20 minutes.   * Serves 6.
* Baking time : 35 minutes.   * Baking temperature : 200°C (400°F).

1½ cups long grained rice, washed and drained
25 mm. (1") stick cinnamon (dalchini)
2 cloves (laung)
1 cup green double beans (Surati papdi)
2 tbsp ghee
salt to taste

To be ground into a paste
½ cup fresh coriander
4 green chillies
1 tsp grated ginger
juice of ½ lemon
¼ cup fresh green garlic (optional)

For serving
Gujarati Kadhi, page 66

1. Heat the ghee in a pan, add the cinnamon and cloves and stir for 30 seconds.
2. Add the rice and stir for a few minutes.
3. Add the beans, the paste, salt and 4 cups of warm water and mix well.
4. Transfer to an earthen pot. Cover and bake in a pre-heated oven at 200°C (400°F) for 30 minutes till the rice is done. Separate each grain of rice lightly with a fork. Serve hot with Gujarati Kadhi.

Handy tips :
1. You can also use cooked rice, if you have any left-over, just remember to also boil the green double beans.
2. If you do not have an earthen pot, use any oven-proof dish instead.

Paneer Pulao

1 cup long grained rice
¼ cup onions, sliced
1 tbsp chopped ginger
1 tbsp chopped garlic
1 tsp green chilli paste
3 tbsp tomato purée
1 cup paneer (cottage cheese), cut into cubes
3 tbsp curds
2 tsp garam masala
2 tbsp chopped coriander
a pinch sugar
1 tbsp oil
salt to taste

1. Clean, wash and soak the rice for approx. 15 minutes. Drain and keep aside.
2. Heat the oil in a pressure cooker, add the onions, ginger, garlic and green chilli

34

paste and stir for a few seconds.

3. Add the tomato purée and paneer cubes and cook for some time.
4. Finally, add the rice, curds, garam masala, coriander, sugar, 2 cups of hot water and salt and pressure cook for 1 whistle.
5. Allow the steam to escape before opening. Separate each grain of rice lightly with fork.

   Serve hot.

Handy tip : You can use chopped tomato instead of tomato purée.

Ghee Rice

Picture on facing page

Preparation time : 10 minutes. ✳ Cooking time : 20 minutes. ✳ Serves 4.

1½ cups long grained rice
25 mm (1") stick cinnamon (dalchini)
3 cloves (laung)
3 cardamoms (elaichi)
1 tsp chopped garlic
1 tsp chopped ginger
1½ cups onions, sliced
¼ cup ghee
salt to taste

For the garnish
fried onions
½ cup fried cashewnuts
2 tbsp fried raisins (kishmis)

Ghee Rice : Recipe above ➜

1. Clean, wash and soak the rice for approx. 15 minutes. Drain and keep aside.
2. Heat the ghee in a pan, add the cinnamon, cardamom, cloves, ginger and garlic and cook for a couple of minutes.
3. Add the onions and cook till they turn golden brown. Remove some onions and keep aside for the garnish.
4. Add the rice and 3½ cups of hot water and salt and pressure cook for 1 whistle. Allow the steam to escape before opening. Separate each grain of rice lightly with a fork. Garnish with the fried onions, cashewnuts and raisins and serve hot.

Lemon Rice

Picture on page 75

‗ Preparation time : 5 minutes. ‗ Cooking time : 10 minutes. ‗ Serves 4.

3 cups steamed rice, page 101
2 whole dry red chillies, broken into pieces
½ tsp mustard seeds (rai)
½ tsp urad dal (split black lentils)
½ tsp grated ginger
1 tsp roasted chana dal (daria)
4 to 5 curry leaves
⅛ tsp turmeric powder (haldi)
juice of ½ lemon
1 tsp oil
salt to taste

For the garnish
few springs of coriander

1. Heat the oil in a non-stick pan and add the red chilies, mustard seeds, urad dal, ginger, chana dal and curry leaves.
2. When the mustard seeds crackle, add the turmeric powder, steamed rice, lemon juice and salt and toss well.

   Serve hot garnished with the sprigs of coriander.

Masoor Biryani

* Preparation time : 30 minutes.   * Cooking time : 10 minutes.   * Serves 4.
* Baking time : 25 minutes.   * Baking temperature : 200°C (400°F).

3 cups steamed rice, page101
¾ cup whole masoor (whole red lentils)
¾ cup onions, sliced
¼ cup onions, chopped
¾ cup tomatoes, chopped
¼ tsp saffron
5 tbsp ghee
oil for deep frying
salt to taste

To be ground into a paste
4 cloves garlic
7 red chillies
3 tsp coriander (dhania) seeds
1½ tsp cumin seeds (jeera)

4 tsp poppy seeds (khus-khus)
25 mm. (1") piece ginger

1. Soak the masoor in water for at least 6 hours. Drain and keep aside.
2. Deep fry the sliced onions in ghee to a golden brown colour. Drain on absorbent paper and keep aside.
3. Heat 3 tablespoons of ghee in a vessel and cook the chopped onions till they turn translucent.
4. Add the paste, fry for a few minutes and then add the tomatoes. Fry for 2 minutes.
5. Add the soaked masoor, salt and ¾ cup of water.
6. Warm the saffron in a small vessel, add 1 teaspoon of milk and rub in till the saffron dissolves.
7. To the cooked rice, add the saffron, fried onions and salt and mix well.
8. In a large baking bowl, put the remaining 2 tbsp of ghee at bottom. Make four layers by spreading ⅓ of the rice, then spreading ½ of the masoor, next spreading a further ⅓ of the rice and finally spreading the remaining masoor and rice.
9. Cover and bake in a pre-heated oven at 200°C (400°F) for 20 minutes. Turn upside down on a big serving plate just before serving.
   Serve hot.

Cabbage Rice

* Preparation time : 10 minutes.   * Cooking time : 20 minutes.   * Serves 4.

3 cups steamed rice, page 101
½ cup onions, grated
1 cup cabbage, shredded
½ cup capsicum, sliced
¼ cup cheese, grated
1 tsp pepper powder
2 tbsp butter
salt to taste

1. Heat the butter in a pan, and sauté the onions for 2 to 3 minutes
2. Add the cabbage and capsicum and cook for 2 to 3 minutes.
3. Add the steamed rice, pepper and salt and mix well.
4. Sprinkle the cheese on top and serve hot.

Handy tip : Approx. 1½ cups of uncooked rice will yield 3 cups of cooked rice.

Korma Rice

✳ Preparation time : 25 minutes. ✳ Cooking time : 20 minutes. ✳ Serves 4.
✳ Baking time : 25 minutes. ✳ Baking temperature : 230°C (450°F).

For the rice
1 cup long grained rice
2 bay leaves (tejpatta)
25 mm. (1") stick cinnamon (dalchini)
2 cardamoms (elaichi)
2 cloves (laung)
2 pinches turmeric powder (haldi)
2 tbsp ghee
salt to taste

For the korma
2 cups whole moong (whole green gram) sprouts
2 tomatoes
2 onions, grated
2 tbsp ginger-garlic paste

1 tsp coriander-cumin seed (dhana-jeera) powder
¼ tsp cardamom (elaichi) powder
1 tsp chilli powder
½ tsp sugar
1 cup milk
2 tbsp fresh cream
3 tbsp ghee
salt to taste

To be ground into cashewnut and poppy seed paste
1 tbsp cashewnuts
1 tbsp poppy seeds (khus-khus)

For baking
1 tbsp ghee

For the rice
1. Clean, wash and soak the rice for approx. 15 minutes. Drain and keep aside.
2. Heat the ghee and fry the bay leaves, cinnamon, cardamoms and cloves and fry for ½ minute.
3. Add the rice, turmeric powder, salt and 4 to 5 cups of water and cook.

4. When the rice is cooked, drain and cool. Each grain of the cooked rice should be separate.

For the korma
1. Boil the tomatoes in hot water. After 10 minutes, remove the skin and chop.
2. Heat the ghee and cook the onions until light pink in colour. Add the ginger-garlic paste, coriander-cumin seed powder, cardamom powder and chilli powder and fry for 1 minute. Add the tomatoes and fry for 3 to 4 minutes.
3. Add the moong sprouts, ¼ cup of water, sugar and salt and cook for a few minutes.
4. In another vessel, mix the milk, cream and cashewnut and poppy seed paste. Add this mixture to the korma and cook for a few minutes.

How to proceed
1. Put 1 tbsp of ghee at the bottom of a baking bowl and build up alternate layers (2 to 3 each depending on the bowl size) of rice and korma, beginning and ending with rice.
2. Cover and bake in a pre-heated oven at 230°C (450°F) for 20 minutes.
3. Just before serving, turn upside down on a serving plate and serve hot.

Masala Bhaat

＊ Preparation time : 15 minutes.   ＊ Cooking time : 20 minutes.   ＊ Serves 4.

1½ cups long grained rice
½ cup brinjals (baingan), diced
½ cup tendli, sliced vertically
a pinch asafoetida (hing)
12 mm. (½") piece ginger, grated
½ tsp turmeric powder (haldi)
½ tsp cumin seeds (jeera)
½ cup onions, chopped
2 green chillies, chopped
1 tsp oil
salt to taste

To be ground into a powder
½ tsp cumin seeds (jeera)
½ tsp coriander (dhania) seeds
8 to 10 peppercorns

3 cloves (laung)

To be mixed into a topping
¼ cup cauliflower, grated
¼ cup coriander, chopped
½ tsp coriander-cumin seed (dhania-jeera) powder
1 tsp chilli powder
½ tsp sugar

1. Clean, wash and soak the rice for approx.15 minutes. Drain and keep aside.
2. Heat the oil in a pressure cooker and add the asafoetida, ginger, turmeric powder and cumin seeds.
3. When the cumin seeds crackle, add the onions and green chillies and sauté till the onions turn translucent.
4. Add the brinjals, tendli and the soaked rice.
5. Add the ground powder, salt with 2½ cups of hot water and pressure cook for 2 to 3 whistles.
6. When the rice is done add the topping mixture and toss well using a fork. Serve hot.

Tamarind Rice

✳ Preparation time : 10 minutes.   ✳ Cooking time : 7 minutes.   ✳ Serves 4.

3 cups steamed rice, page 101
1 tbsp urad dal (split black lentils)
1 green chilli, slit
1 whole dry red chilli, broken into pieces
1 tsp grated ginger
¼ tsp asafoetida (hing)
6 to 8 curry leaves
2 tbsp oil
salt to taste

For the tamarind paste
¼ cup tamarind (imli)
¼ tsp turmeric powder (haldi)
½ tsp chilli powder
½ cup water

For the garnish
1 tbsp ghee
1 tbsp chopped coriander

For the tamarind paste
1. Combine the tamarind with ½ cup of water and cook over medium flame for a minute. Allow it to cool slightly.
2. Pass through a strainer to get a thick pulp.
3. Add the turmeric powder and chilli powder and keep aside.

For the rice
1. Heat the oil in a pan and add the urad dal and roast till it turns golden brown in colour.
2. Add the green chilli, dry red chilli, ginger, asafoetida and curry leaves and cook for a few more seconds.
3. Add the tamarind paste, mix well and cook for 2 minutes.
4. Add the steamed rice and salt, mix well and cook for 3 to 4 minutes.
   Serve hot garnished with the ghee and coriander.

Aloo Gobi Ka Pulao

Picture on page 65

✳ Preparation time : 10 minutes. ✳ Cooking time : 20 minutes. ✳ Serves 4.

1½ cups long grained rice
1 cup potatoes, cut into cubes
1 cup cauliflower, cut into florets
2 bay leaves (tejpatta)
5 to 6 cloves (laung)
25 mm. (1") cinnamon (dalchini)
2 tsp turmeric powder (haldi)
¼ tsp dry ginger powder (soonth)
1 tsp chilli powder
1 tsp garam masala powder
2 tbsp oil
salt to taste

For the garnish
a few mint sprigs

1. Clean, wash and soak the rice for approx. 15 minutes. Drain and keep aside.
2. Heat the oil in a pressure cooker and add the bay leaves, cloves and cinnamon.
3. When they crackle, add the turmeric powder, dry ginger powder, chilli powder, garam masala powder, potatoes and cauliflower.
4. Sauté for 2 minutes and then add the rice.
5. Sauté for 2 more minutes, add 3 cups of hot water and salt and pressure cook for 1 whistle.
6. Allow the steam to escape before opening. Separate each grain of rice very lightly with a fork.
   Garnish with the mint springs and serve hot.

Pearl Pulao

Picture on page 55

* Preparation time : 15 minutes.   * Cooking time : 50 minutes.   * Serves 4.

1 cup brown rice
½ cup baby onions
½ cup whole baby garlic
25 mm. (1") stick cinnamon (dalchini)
2 cloves (laung)
1 bay leaf (tejpatta)
1 cardamom (elaichi)
½ cup fresh cream
¼ cup cheese, grated
3 tbsp oil
salt to taste

1. Clean, wash and soak the rice for 4 to 5 hours. Drain and keep aside.
2. Heat the oil in a pan, add the onions and garlic and sauté till they are golden brown.
3. Add the cinnamon, cloves, bay leaf and cardamom and sauté for 1 minute.

53

4. Add the rice and salt and sauté for a further 3 to 4 minutes.
5. Add 2½ cups of hot water, cover the pan with the lid and simmer on a slow flame till the rice is 80% cooked.
6. Add the cream and cheese, cover with a lid and cook on a very slow flame till the rice absorbs all the liquid.
7. Separate each grain of rice very lightly with a fork.
   Serve hot.

Handy tip : Certain varieties of brown rice require a much longer soaking time and also absorb a lot more water when cooking.

Pearl Pulao : Recipe on page 53 ↝

Khichadi

Panchamel Khichadi

✳ Preparation time : 15 minutes. ✳ Cooking time : 15 minutes. ✳ Serves 4.

1½ cups long grained rice
1 tbsp masoor dal (split red lentils)
1 tbsp chana dal (split Bengal gram)
1 tbsp yellow moong dal (split yellow lentils)
1 tbsp toovar (arhar) dal
1 tsp cumin seeds (jeera)
1 tsp finely chopped garlic
1 tsp grated ginger
¼ cup onions, cut into cubes
½ cup cabbage, cut into big pieces
¾ cup cauliflower, cut into florets
½ cup potatoes, peeled and chopped
½ cup green peas
1 tsp chilli powder
¼ tsp turmeric powder (haldi)
2 tsp coriander (dhania) powder

½ cup tomatoes, chopped
2 tbsp ghee
salt to taste

1. Clean, wash and soak the rice and dals for approx. 15 minutes. Drain and keep aside.
2. Heat the ghee in a pressure cooker and add the cumin seeds.
3. When the seeds crackle, add the garlic and ginger and sauté for 1 minute.
4. Add the onions and sauté till the onions turn translucent.
5. Add the cabbage, cauliflower, potatoes and peas and sauté for some time.
6. Add the chilli powder, turmeric powder, coriander powder and stir again.
7. Add the tomatoes and sauté for some more time.
8. Add the rice and dals, 3 cups of hot water and salt and pressure cook for 2 whistles.
9. Allow the steam to escape before opening.
   Serve hot.

Badshahi Khichadi

* Preparation time : 10 minutes.   * Cooking time : 30 minutes.   * Serves 4.

For the rice
1 cup ambe mohar rice
½ cup toovar (arhar) dal
2 cloves (laung)
25 mm. (1") stick cinnamon (dalchini)
a pinch asafoetida (hing)
¼ tsp turmeric powder (haldi)
2 tbsp ghee
salt to taste

For the potato vegetable
4 medium sized potatoes, boiled, peeled and cut into cubes
1 tsp mustard seeds (rai)
1 tsp ginger-green chilli paste
½ cup onions, sliced
¼ tsp turmeric powder (haldi)

1 tsp chilli powder
1 tsp coriander (dhania) powder
3 tbsp fresh curds
2 tbsp ghee
salt to taste

For the tempered curds
1 cup fresh curds
1 tsp mustard seeds (rai)
4 to 6 curry leaves
1 tsp ghee
salt to taste

For the garnish
2 tbsp chopped coriander

For.the rice
1. Clean, wash and soak the rice and toovar dal for approx. 15 minutes. Drain and keep aside.
2. Heat the ghee in a pressure cooker, add the cloves and cinnamon and stir-fry for half a minute. Add the asafoetida and turmeric powder. Mix well.

3. Add the rice, toovar dal, salt and 4 cups of hot water and pressure cook for 2 whistles till the rice is slightly over-cooked.
4. Allow the steam to escape before opening. Keep aside.

For the potato vegetable
1. Heat the ghee in a pan and add the mustard seeds to it. When the seeds crackle, add the onions and fry for some time till they turn translucent.
2. Add the ginger-green chilli paste, turmeric powder, chilli powder and coriander powder and sauté for 1 to 2 minutes.
3. Add the potatoes and salt and sauté for some more time.
4. Add the curds, mix well and keep aside.

For the tempered curds
1. Whisk the curds with salt and keep aside.
2. Heat the ghee in a small pan and add the mustard seeds to it.
3. When they crackle, add the curry leaves and pour over the curds. Mix well.

How to proceed
1. Place the potato vegetable at the bottom of a serving dish.
2. Top with a layer of the rice over it.
3. Pour the curds on top and garnish with the chopped coriander.
   Serve immediately.

Wholesome Khichadi

* Preparation time : 10 minutes.   * Cooking time : 25 minutes.   * Serves 4.

⅔ cup ambe mohar rice
⅔ cup yellow moong dal (split yellow gram)
1 cup bottle gourd (doodhi/lauki), grated
1 cup carrot, grated
½ tsp turmeric powder (haldi)
1 tsp cumin seeds (jeera)
½ tsp asafoetida (hing)
6 peppercorns
1 bay leaf (tejpatta)
4 cloves (laung)
½ tbsp ghee
salt to taste

For serving
fresh curds

1. Clean, wash and soak the rice and moong dal for approx. 15 minutes. Drain and keep aside.
2. Heat the ghee in a pressure cooker, and add the cumin seeds. When they crackle, add the asafoetida, peppercorns, bay leaf and cloves.
3. Add the bottle gourd and carrot and sauté for a few seconds.
4. Add the dal, rice, turmeric powder, salt and 3 cups of water and pressure cook for 3 whistles.
5. Allow the steam to escape before opening.
6. Whisk the khichadi lightly to combine the rice and dal together.
   Serve hot with fresh curds.

Handi Khichadi

* Preparation time : 30 minutes. * Cooking time : 30 minutes. * Serves 6.
* Baking time : 30 minutes. * Baking temperature : 200°C (400°F).

1½ cups rice
1½ cups papadi beans (leelva)
1½ cups Guajrati kadhi, recipe below
50 mm. (2") stick cinnamon (dalchini)
3 cloves (laung)
2 bay leaves (tejpatta)
3 tbsp ghee
salt to taste

To be ground into a paste
¼ cup onions, chopped
6 green chillies
25 mm. (1") piece ginger
2 cardamoms (elaichi)

Aloo Gobi Ka Pulao : Recipe on page 51 →

1 tsp lemon juice
3 tbsp chopped coriander
6 cloves garlic

For the Gujarati kadhi
2 tbsp Bengal gram flour (besan)
2 cups fresh curds
1 tsp chilli-ginger paste
2 curry leaves
2 tablespoons sugar (approx.)
2 tablespoons chopped coriander
salt to taste

For the tempering of Gujarati kadhi
½ tsp cumin seeds (jeera)
½ tsp mustard seeds (rai)
a pinch asafoetida (hing)
1 whole dry red chilli, broken into pieces
2 tsp ghee

For the kadhi
1. Mix the gram flour, curds and 2 cups of water. Beat well.
2. Add the chilli-ginger paste, curry leaves, sugar and salt and put to boil while stirring at intervals.
3. Boil whilst stirring for a while.
4. Prepare the tempering by heating the ghee and frying the cumin and mustard seeds until they turn brown. Add the asafoetida and dry red chilli.
5. Add the tempering to the kadhi and boil for a few minutes. Keep hot.

How to proceed
1. Heat the ghee in a pan and fry the cinnamon, cloves and bay leaves for a few seconds.
2. Add the paste and fry for 2 minutes.
3. Add the rice and beans and cook for 2 minutes
4. Add 4 cups of hot water and salt and pour the mixture into an earthen pot (or a big bowl).
5. Cover and cook in a pre-heated oven at 200°C (400°F) for 20 minutes.
6. When the rice is cooked, pour the kadhi over it.
7. Cover and bake again at 200°C (400°F) for 5 minutes.
   Serve hot.

Ek Top Na Dal Bhaat

＊ Preparation time : 20 minutes.　　＊ Cooking time : 40 minutes.　　＊ Serves 6.

1½ cups short grained rice
¾ cup toovar (arhar) dal
2 to 3 pinches asafoetida (hing)
2 pinches soda-bi-carb
¼ teaspoon turmeric powder (haldi)
10 small onions
5 small potatoes
4 to 5 small brinjals
¾ cup green peas
4 tbsp ghee

To be mixed together into a masala mixture
4 tsp coriander-cumin seed (dhania-jeera) powder
4 tsp sugar
2 tsp chilli powder
½ grated fresh coconut

4 to 5 tbsp chopped coriander
a pinch asafoetida (hing)
salt to taste

For serving
ghee
buttermilk

1. Make criss-cross slits on the onions, potatoes and brinjals, taking care not to separate the segments. Stuff the slits with the masala mixture. About half the mixture will remain.
2. Clean, wash and soak the rice and dal separately for approx. 15 minutes. Drain and keep aside.
3. Heat the ghee in a pan, add the asafoetida and the toovar dal and fry for 2 minutes. Add the soda-bi-carb, turmeric powder and 2 cups of water. Cover and cook for at least 5 to 7 minutes.
4. Spread the vegetables, cover with the rice and continue cooking.
5. In another vessel, heat about 2 cups of water and add 1 tablespoon of salt and pinch of turmeric powder. Pour this water, a little at a time, over the rice. Cook until the rice is done.
6. Sprinkle the remaining masala mixture over the rice. Mix lightly.
Serve hot with ghee and buttermilk.

Handy tips :

1. Stir this as little as possible otherwise the vegetables will break.
2. A rice cooker may be used to make this recipe.

Bisi Bele Huli Anna

＊ Preparation time : 20 minutes.　　＊ Cooking time : 30 minutes.　　＊ Serves 4.

1 cup toovar (arhar) dal (washed)
1 cup uncooked rice (washed)
¼ cup French beans, chopped
¼ cup carrots, chopped
½ cup potatoes, cut into 25 mm. (1") cubes
½ cup capsicums, cut into 25 mm. (1") cubes
½ tsp turmeric powder (haldi)
3 curry leaves
2 tbsp tamarind pulp
2 tsp oil
salt to taste

For the powdered masala
2 tbsp chana dal (split Bengal gram)
2 tbsp urad dal (split black lentils)
25 mm (1") sticks cinnamon (dalchini)

71

½ dry coconut
8 whole dry red chillies
3 tbsp coriander (dhania) seeds
1 tbsb oil

1. Boil the vegetables and keep aside.
2. Boil 5 cups of water in a heavy-bottomed pan, add the oil, turmeric powder, toovar dal and salt and cook for 5 to 6 minutes.
3. Add the rice, cover and cook over medium flame for 20 minutes, till the rice and dal are cooked.

For the powdered masala
1. Heat the oil and roast all the ingredients except the coconut, blend in a blender to a fine powder.
2. Powder the coconut separately.

How to proceed
When the rice is cooked, add the boiled vegetables, powdered masala, curry leaves, tamarind pulp and salt, mix gently and cook for further 5 minutes.
Serve hot with ghee.

Coriander Curd Rice

✳ Preparation time : 10 minutes.   ✳ Cooking time : 15 minutes.   ✳ Serves 4.

3 cups steamed rice, page 101, cooled
1 cup fresh curds
¼ cup chopped coriander
salt to taste

For the tempering
1 dry red chilli, broken into pieces
2 tsp urad dal (split black lentils)
1 tsp mustard seeds (rai)
¼ tsp asafoetida (hing)
2 tbsp ghee or oil

1. Mix together the rice, curds and salt and mash well. You could also blend it slightly in a mixer to make a rough purée.
2. Heat the ghee in a small pan and add the mustard seeds.
3. When the seeds crackle, add the urad dal, red chilli and asafoetida.

73

4. Add this to the mashed rice and curd mixture.
5. Add salt and coriander and mix well.
   Refrigerate and serve cold.

Lemon Rice : Recipe on page 39 ➔

Chitrana Rice

✳ Preparation time : 20 minutes.   ✳ Cooking time : 10 minutes.   ✳ Serves 4.

1½ cups short grained rice
3 tbsp peanuts
3 tbsp sesame seeds (til)
1 tbsp chana dal (split Bengal gram)
½ tsp mustard seeds (rai)
3 whole dry red chillies
5 curry leaves
¼ tsp asafoetida (hing)
2 tbsp grated fresh coconut
3 tbsp tamarind pulp
2 tbsp malagapadi powder, recipe overleaf
¼ tsp turmeric powder (haldi)
2 tbsp ghee
salt to taste

For the malagapadi powder
2 tbsp coriander (dhania) seeds
1½ tbsp cumin seeds (jeera)
2 tbsp chana dal (split Bengal gram)
2 tbsp urad dal (split black lentils)
2 tbsp sesame seeds (til)
12 whole dry red chillies
1 tsp asafoetida (hing)
1 tsp salt

For the malagapadi powder
Mix and dry roast all the ingredients. When roasted, powder and store in an air-tight container.

How to proceed
1. Clean, wash and soak the rice for approx. 15 minutes. Drain and keep aside.
2. Boil 5 cups of water, add the rice and cook till the rice is done, each grain of the cooked rice should be separate. Drain and discard the water and cool the rice.
3. Roast the peanuts and sesame seeds separately and powder them coarsely.
4. Heat the ghee, add the chana dal and mustard seeds and roast for 1 minute.
5. Add the dry red chillies, curry leaves and asafoetida and cook for further ½ minute.

6. Finally, add the cooked rice, coconut, tamarind pulp, turmeric powder, malagapadi powder, roasted peanuts, sesame seeds and salt and cook for a few minutes.
Serve hot.

Handi Hot Pot

* Preparation time : 30 minutes.　　* Cooking time : 40 minutes.　　* Serves 4.

1 cup long grained rice
½ cup cauliflower, cut into florets
½ cup potatoes, cut into 25 mm. (1") cubes
½ cup green peas
½ cup onions, chopped
½ cup coriander, chopped
½ tsp turmeric powder (haldi)
4 tsp coriander-cumin seed (dhania-jeera) powder
1 tsp chilli powder
1 tsp garam masala
4 tbsp oil
salt to taste

To be ground into a paste
4 tbsp grated fresh coconut
4 green chillies

25 mm. (1″) piece ginger
14 cloves garlic

For the garnish
2 tbsp chopped coriander

1. Mix the onions, coriander, turmeric powder, coriander-cumin seed powder, chilli powder, garam masala, prepared paste, oil and salt very well.
2. Add the cauliflower, potatoes, peas and rice to this mixture and mix thoroughly.
3. Put in a big handi, add 3 cups of hot water, cover and cook until the vegetables are cooked.
   garnish with the chopped coriander and serve hot.

International Favourites

Roasted Vegetables With Brown Rice

⁎ Preparation time : 15 minutes.   ⁎ Cooking time : 15 minutes.   ⁎ Serves 4.
⁎ Baking time : 40 minutes.   ⁎ Baking temperature : 200°C (400°F).

For the brown rice
1 cup brown rice
½ cup onions, sliced
2 cloves garlic, chopped
2 tbsp olive oil or oil
salt to taste

For the vegetables
3 cups mixed vegetables (broccoli, carrots, red and green capsicum, baby corn), cut
into 25 mm. (1") pieces
4 cloves garlic, chopped
1 tbsp olive oil or oil
salt to taste

For the cheese sauce
2 tbsp plain flour (maida)
2 tbsp butter
2 cups milk
1 tsp chilli flakes
½ cup cheese, grated
½ tsp dried mixed herbs
salt and pepper to taste

For the brown rice
1. Clean, wash and soak the rice for 4 to 5 hours. Drain and keep aside.
2. Heat the olive oil in a pan, add the onions and sauté till they turn translucent. Add the garlic and sauté for another 2 minutes.
3. Add the rice and salt and sauté for a further 3 to 4 minutes.
4. Add 3 cups of hot water, cover the pan with a lid and simmer on a slow flame till the rice is cooked. Separate each grain of rice lightly with a fork.

For the roasted vegetables
1. Combine the vegetables, garlic, olive oil and salt in a baking tray. Toss well.
2. Bake in pre-heated oven at 200°C (400°F) for 15 to 20 minutes, stirring once in between till they are slightly brown in colour. Keep aside.

For the cheese sauce
1. Melt the butter in a pan, add the flour and sauté for 1 minute.
2. Gradually, add the milk and 1 cup of water, stirring continuously so that no lumps form. Bring to a boil.
3. Remove from the fire, add the chilli flakes, cheese, mixed herbs, salt and pepper and stir well. Keep aside.

How to proceed
1. Arrange a layer of the brown rice in a 200 mm. (8") diameter baking dish.
2. Cover with a layer of the roasted vegetables and top with the cheese sauce.
3. Just before serving, bake in a pre-heated oven at 220°C (430°F) for 10 to 15 minutes. Serve hot.

Handy tip : Certain varieties of brown rice require a much longer soaking time and also absorb a lot more water when cooking.

Steamed Curry Rice : Recipe on page 86 →

Steamed Curry Rice

Picture on page 85

✳ Preparation time : 15 minute.   ✳ Cooking time : 15 minute.   ✳ Serves 4.

3 cups steamed rice, page 101
2 tbsp garlic paste
1 tbsp red chilli paste
½ cup coconut milk, page 102
¼ cup French beans, sliced diagonally and boiled
¼ cup green peas, boiled
¼ cup baby corn, boiled and sliced
1 tbsp finely chopped fresh basil
1 tsp lemon rind
½ banana leaf
2 tbsp olive oil
salt to taste

1. Heat the olive oil, add the garlic paste and red chilli paste and cook for 3 to 4 minutes.
2. Add the coconut milk, all the boiled vegetables, basil, lemon rind and salt and

bring the coconut milk to a boil.
3. Add the rice and mix well.
4. Turn this flavoured rice onto the centre of a banana leaf (kitchen foil can be used as substitute).
5. Fold the leaf into a square packet and steam in a steamer till done.

Handy tip : Red chilli paste is made by soaking dry red chillies in lukewarm water for about 15 minutes and then grinding it to a fine paste.

Thai Layered Rice

＊ Preparation time : 15 minutes.   ＊ Cooking time : 10 minutes.   ＊ Serves 4.
＊ Baking time : 25 minutes.   ＊ Baking temperature : 200°C (400°F).

For the rice
1 cup long grained rice
1 cup coconut milk, page 102
4 tsp chopped coriander
1 tsp salt
1 tsp oil

For the vegetable curry
1 cup broccoli, cut into florets
8 babycorn, sliced diagonally
½ pineapple, peeled and cored
2 tbsp garlic paste
2 tbsp red chilli paste
1 tsp cornflour
1 cup coconut milk, page 102

2 tbsp lemon juice
2 tsp sugar
1 tbsp soya sauce
rind of 1 lemon, grated
2 tbsp chopped fresh basil
2 tbsp oil
salt to taste

For the garnish
2 tbsp sliced onions, fried till brown
2 tbsp chopped spring onions

Other ingredients
½ cup plain flour (maida)

For the rice
1. Clean, wash and soak the rice for approx. 15 minutes. Drain and keep aside.
2. Heat the oil in a pan, add the rice and sauté for 4 to 5 minutes.
3. Add the coconut milk, 1 cup of water and the salt.
4. Bring to a boil, cover the pan with a lid and cook till the rice is 80% done.
5. Separate each grain of rice very lightly with a fork.
6. Sprinkle the coriander on top and keep aside.

For the vegetable curry

1. Blanch the broccoli and babycorn in hot water. Drain and keep aside.
2. Cut the pineapple into 25 mm. (1") cubes, keep aside.
3. Heat the oil in a pan, add the garlic and chilli pastes and fry for a few minutes.
4. Mix the cornflour in the coconut milk and add to the above mixture.
5. Add the blanched vegetables and the pineapple to the gravy.
6. Add the lemon juice, sugar, soya sauce, lemon rind, basil and salt.
7. Bring to a boil and keep aside.

How to proceed

1. Make a dough with the flour and water. This will be used to seal the edges of the pan in which the rice is made. Keep aside.
2. In a flat-bottomed pan, spread a layer of rice and top with a layer of the vegetable curry.
3. Repeat the layers till all the rice and vegetable curry are used.
4. Cover with a lid and seal the sides with the maida dough.
5. Bake in a pre-heated oven at 200°C (400°F) for 20 minutes.
6. Remove from the oven and break the seal.
   Serve hot garnished with the brown onions and spring onions.

Handy tip : To make red chilli paste, soak dry red chillies in lukewarm water for about 15 minutes and then grind to a smooth paste.

Mexican Fried Rice

＊ Preparation time : 30 minutes.　　＊ Cooking time : 30 minutes.　　＊ Serves 6.

3 cups steamed rice, page 101
½ cup onions, sliced
3 cloves garlic, crushed
¼ tsp turmeric powder (haldi)
¼ cup capsicum, sliced
¼ cup tomatoes, chopped
1 cup mixed boiled vegetables (French beans, carrots, green peas)
1 tsp chilli powder
6 tbsp oil
salt to taste

1. Heat the oil in a broad vessel and fry the onions until golden brown in colour.
2. Remove the onions and place on absorbent paper.
3. In the same oil, fry the capsicum for 1 minute.
4. Add the garlic and fry for a few seconds. Add the turmeric powder and fry again for a few seconds.

5. Add the tomatoes, boiled vegetables, chilli powder and salt and cook for 1 minute.
6. Add the fried onions and the steamed rice and mix well.
   Serve hot.

Chinese Fried Rice

∗ Preparation time : 15 minutes.　　∗ Cooking time : 30 minutes.　　∗ Serves 4.

3 cups steamed rice, page 101
¾ cup French beans, cut diagonally into thin strips
¾ cup carrots, cut into long thin strips
¾ cup capsicum, cut into long thin strips
1 tbsp chopped celery
½ cup spring onion whites, chopped
2 tsp soya sauce
1½ cups spring onion greens, chopped
a pinch Mono Sodium Glutamate (MSG) (optional)
1 tbsp oil
salt to taste

1. Heat the oil in a pan, add the vegetables, celery, spring onion whites and MSG and sauté over a high flame for 3 to 4 minutes till the vegetables soften.
2. Add the rice, soya sauce, spring onion greens and salt. Mix well and sauté for 2 minutes.
   Serve hot.

Risotto Florentina

＊Preparation time : 10 minutes.   ＊Cooking time : 20 minutes.   ＊Serves 4.

1 cup long grained rice
¼ cup carrots, finely chopped
¼ cup green peas
1 tsp chopped garlic
1 cup spinach (palak), blanched, drained and finely chopped
2 tbsp chopped fresh basil
2 tbsp finely chopped celery
1 tbsp finely chopped parsley
½ cup cheese, grated
⅓ cup tomato purée
2 tbsp fresh cream
2 to 3 tbsp red wine (optional)
3 tbsp olive oil or oil
salt to taste

1. Clean, wash and soak the rice for about 10 minutes. Drain and keep aside.
2. Heat the olive oil in a pan, add the carrots, green peas and garlic and sauté for 2 minutes.
3. Add the rice and sauté for 2 minutes.
4. Pour 3½ cups of hot water and salt and bring to a boil. Cover and simmer till the rice is 80% done, adding a little water if required.
5. When the rice is cooked, add the spinach, basil, celery, parsley, cheese, tomato purée, cream and red wine and mix well.
   Serve immediately.

Handy tips :
1. Toss in the greens (i.e. spinach, basil and parsley) just before you are ready to serve the risotto or they will discolour.
2. A risotto should have the consistency and texture of a khichadi.

Spanish Rice

* Preparation time : 15 minutes.   * Cooking time : 40 minutes.   * Serves 4.
    * Baking time : 15 minutes.   * Baking temperature : 200°C (400°F).

1 cup long grained rice
¼ cup French beans, chopped
¼ cup potatoes, cut into cubes
¼ cup carrots, chopped
¼ cup green peas, boiled
½ cup onions, chopped
½ cup capsicum, chopped
¼ cup tomatoes, deseeded and cut into cubes
2 tbsp curds
1 tsp garam masala
10 cloves garlic
5 whole dry chillies
6 tbsp oil
salt to taste

For the garnish
tomatoes slices
4 tbsp grated cooking cheese

1. Clean, wash and soak the rice for approx. 15 minutes. Drain and keep aside.
2. Boil 4 cups of water, add the rice and cook till the rice is 80% done, each grain of the rice should be separate. Drain and discard the water and cool the rice.
3. Roast the chillies on a frying pan for a few minutes. Pound with the garlic and keep aside.
4. Heat the oil in a pan, add the onions and fry for 1 minute.
5. Add the pounded garlic and chillies and fry for 2 minutes.
6. Add the capsicum, tomatoes and curds and cook for another 4 minutes.
7. Add the cooked rice, salt, vegetables and garam masala and mix well.
8. Grease a baking dish and pack the rice in it.
9. Garnish with tomato slices and the grated cheese.
10. Bake in a pre-heated oven at 200°C (400°F) for 10 minutes.
    Serve hot.

Desserts

Sitafal Firni

* Preparation time : 15 minutes.   * Cooking time : 20 minutes.   * Serves 4.

1 litre full fat milk
½ cup rice, soaked for 2 hours
4 to 6 tablespoons sugar
1½ cups custard apple (sitafal) pulp, deseeded

1. Drain out the water from the rice.
2. Make a smooth paste by blending together the soaked rice and ½ cup of cold milk.
3. Mix this in the remaining milk and sugar and bring to a boil over a medium flame, stirring continuously.
4. Simmer for 5 to 10 minutes till the mixture thickens and the rice is cooked.
5. Cool completely and add the custard apple pulp.
6. Mix well and chill for 3 to 4 hours.
   Serve chilled.

Rice Kheer

* Preparation time : 5 minutes.   * Cooking time : 15 minutes.   * Serves 4.

1 cup steamed rice, page 101
2 cups full fat milk
⅓ cup condensed milk
2 tbsp sugar
½ tsp cardamom (elaichi) powder
1 tsp ghee

1. Mix together the steamed rice, milk and condensed milk in a broad non-stick pan and simmer on a flame, stirring continuously, for about 10 minutes.
2. Add the sugar, cardamom powder and ghee and mix well till the sugar dissolves. Serve hot.

Handy tip : The rice should be over-cooked to get a more creamy texture for the kheer.

Steamed Rice

✳ Preparation time : 5 minutes. ✳ Cooking time : 15 minutes. ✳ Makes 3 cups.

1½ cups long grained rice
2 tbsp oil
1 tsp salt

1. Wash the rice thoroughly and soak in 3 cups of water for 30 minutes. Drain and keep aside.
2. Boil 6 to 8 cups of water, add salt and 1 tbsp of oil.
3. Add the rice to the boiling water. Cook till the rice is 85% cooked.
4. Pour into a colander and let the water drain out. Pour some cold water on the rice to arrest further cooking.
5. Let all the water from the rice drain out ensuring that the rice does not contain any moisture.

6. Add the remaining 1 tbsp of oil and toss the rice in it
7. Spread the cooked rice on a flat surface till it is cool.
   Use as required.

Handy tip : A colander is a perforated vessel that is used to drain out the water when cooking rice and also to wash vegetables.

Coconut Milk

✳ Preparation time : 10 minutes.   ✳ No cooking.   ✳ Makes 2½ to 3 cups.

1 fresh coconut, grated
2 cups warm water

Mix the coconut and warm water and allow it to stand for 2 hours and then strain using a muslin cloth. The strained liquid is coconut milk.

Handy tip : Carefully grate only the white part of the coconut avoiding the brown skin as it will change the colour of the milk.

Mini Series by *Tarla Dalal*

Healthy Breakfast

Healthy Snacks

Healthy
Soups & Salads

Healthy Juices

Fast Foods
Made Healthy

Calcium
Rich Recipes

Iron Rich Recipes

Forever Young Diet

Home Remedies

Low Cholesterol
Recipes